Moss.

Volume Seven.

M. A publication of Moss.
https://mosslit.com

© 2022 Moss: a Journal of the Pacific Northwest
407 W. Howe St.
Seattle, WA 98119

Twitter: @mosslitmag
mosslit@gmail.com

Abortion is a human right.

"#ClimbingNation" © Kim Fu. From *Lesser Known Monsters of the 21st Century*.
Reprinted with permission from Tin House.

Cover photo © 2017 Alex Davis-Lawrence. Interior photos as credited,
used under a Creative Commons Attribution-only license (CC BY 2.0).

Printing by Bookmobile Printing Services
ISBN: 978-0-9969379-6-2

Printed in the United States of America
1 4 5 2 9 10 8 6 3 0

About Moss.

Moss is a literary journal of the Pacific Northwest. Founded in 2014, *Moss* is dedicated to exploring the intersection of place and creative expression while exposing the region's outstanding writers to a broad audience of readers, critics, and publishers.

Contents.

Fiction

Old Ladies of the Woods, Matt Briggs	3
#ClimbingNation, Kim Fu	23
Dash, Aaron Fullerton	51
A La Fuerza, Maria de Lourdes Victoria	91
The Bubble, Max Delsohn	95
Cabin Life, Jennifer Fernandez	115
Still Living Things, David Naimon	125
La Forestal, Rita Sturam Wirkala	169

Non-fiction

Machines, Keygan S. S. McClellan	37
Glory Glory Hallelujah, Katherine D. Morgan	49
Door Stoop, CMarie Fuhrman	161

Interviews

Kim Fu with Kailee Haong	11
Oliver de la Paz with The Poet Salon	75
Sayantani Dasgupta with Tara Roberts	151
Angela Garbes with Alayna Becker	201

Poetry

Remaindered, Nanya Jhingran	1
Reading the Book of Isaiah While Wild Fires Continue to Burn, Jory Mickelson	47
Monuments for Men (Memory's Vault), Fort Worden, Shin Yu Pai	89
Prayer for Trimet Line 17, Jaye Nasir	111
Futures, Ayana Harscoet	165
The Boys of Boise 1955, Alex Vigue	199
Little North Fork, Joe Wilkins	225

Contributors 227
Acknowledgments 235

In my own writing,
my goal has been to make the body undeniable,
so that when you're reading it,
you have physical sensation...
you might feel some of those things in your body.

Angela Garbes

520 Bridge under construction, 1962.
Engineering Department (Record Series 2613-07), Seattle Municipal Archives.

Remaindered
Nanya Jhingran

On the bus to work, craning my neck into shaky gaps
        between swaying professionals, I catch hungry glimpses

of the unfinished horizon, throw wide the net of my sight
                      beyond the middle distance.

Sheet metal's glint off downtown's crane-brushed canopy,
              birds periodically smashed into glass,

that mauled vulture I saw beside my Amtrak to Portland, or

whatever remains of the grotesque once swallowed by the ordinary.
        All afternoon laundered suits swish in & out of
              meeting rooms, & crooning of profit and loss

drown the noises rising from the street outside.

What hangs in the balance?

Even on the sunny days, I can never see

what lies on the other side of the ridged treeline.

Old Ladies of the Woods
Matt Briggs

My mother sits on the couch in the living room wrapped in an afghan she and my grandmother crocheted over Christmas. My grandmother tested the ratio of the gaps in the brown and orange and yellow yarn with the width of a number two pencil. While crocheting my grandmother took breaks from knitting to bake cookies. My mother took a break to make sandwiches. I put together a winter puzzle on the coffee table. They told family stories on the couch over the tap of the hooks. The afghan smelled fresh then, like detergent. I could have a cookie. And then the second cookie was a trade. I had to chop the firewood for the week. One cookie for a handful of blisters. A cookie now and then a week from now, blisters.

By the spring when I could finally go outside and the windows had been open, the afghan carried the smell of my grandmother's living room cedar oil candles, which she lit to keep out the moths, my grandfather's pipe, my mother's cigarettes, and my father's joints. The fabric held the smell like a memory among the number two pencil gaps. Fabric remembers things. Old clothes know where they have been worn. My hand-me-down jacket that had fallen out of use before I was born. It was a longshoreman's jacket. "What happened to him?"

"Who?"

"The longshoreman who wore this jacket?"

"I don't know who owned your jacket. They took good care of it."

Mom bought me a shirt from the Salvation Army. I told her that the boy who wore it before me died. "Don't say that" Mom said. "You don't know that."

"I know I don't know," I said. "The shirt knows. The shirt remembers."

"If anything happened to you," Mom said, "I wouldn't sell your shirts to a secondhand store."

"Something happened to this boy," I said. "And look now. I got his shirt. Something useful came out of it."

"Don't say that," Mom said. "Tell me if anything happens to you. I'll make sure nothing bad happens to you."

"I don't know how," I said. "But I'll tell you before something bad happens to me if something bad happens to me."

"Don't say that. It's creepy."

If I caught a deadly flu, I would just wither away in bed. I can imagine laying among the tangled sheets in drowsy agony. I would hate that because Mom would do everything in her power to make sure I didn't die.

She said she gave birth to me and that made everything in her life have meaning. This made me think of myself as an answer and of her as a question. Do all answers feel such responsibility to their questions?

This flu is lethal. It fills my lungs with mucus. My head swims with mobs of germs. Mom bombards me with the menthol goo of Vik's Vapo-Rub. She soaks me in salts and medicinal packs. And yet there is nothing she can do. I could die even if I was bathed in Vik's. That would be a relief from the entire bubble boy world Mom keeps me in. It makes sense that she would keep me wrapped up like a porcelain plate waiting for the dinner that never got set out on its surface.

When the rain really breaks in the spring, and the days become clear enough, I take off to the forest. Mom is under the afghan again. She has a cigarette and her pack at the ready on the arm of the couch. She reads from the pile of paperbacks she got from the paperback exchange. She looks up. "Stay in earshot," she says. "I call, you come."

"I will come if I can hear you. But I might not be able to hear you."

"Don't say that," she says, "I call, you come in straight to the house."

The first time she calls, I make sure I run headfirst into the nettles between the stand of cedar trees I like to play in and the house. I make sure I run straight through those nettles. They smell leafy like a salad or the long grass on the cattle pasture above the house. The leaves bite. They have tiny hooks on the edge of the shovel-shaped leaves. The leaves drape and then cling to my skin and leave acid stings that immediately turn white with a ring of inflamed flesh. Each one is like a hard pinch that stays pinched. Mom calls my name and I plow through those nettles. I go through them, and I have welts everywhere. I have welts on my belly button. I have welts in the fold of skin between my index finger and middle finger. I have welts in my ear canal. I stagger into the house.

"What took you so long?"

"It's dangerous for me to just come in a straight line to the house," I tell her. "The forest is full of dangers like nettles."

"Didn't you feel that they were stinging you? You're stung everywhere."

I stagger around the room. "It's like getting a burn," I say. "It is just like getting a burn. If you get a burn over 80% of your body, you die."

Mom has to step away from her afghan. She stands in the middle of the kitchen. "We can treat this. Quick," she says, "into the bathtub."

She fills the tub with warm rather than hot water. After I wash, she takes a bottle of calamine lotion and dabs a drop on each welt. She gives me a tiny white pill, the one I take when I have hay fever. It seems like it should be sweet, but instead it just vanishes on my tongue with a faint chemical aftertaste. She continues to dab the lotion on me. Finally, she sets me down on the bed. "You need to have sense in this world," she says. "You are precious to me. I don't know what I would do if I lost you."

"You need to let me make my own decisions," I say.

"You can make your own decisions as soon as I know they would be the decision I would make," she says. "You can't go off and pull stunts like this."

"I just want—" but the hay fever medicine puts me to sleep. I wake hours later, and the rain has come back. My father works nights. During the day he goes fishing or hiking or works at the horse ranch at the bottom of the hill. That is why we moved to the house in the forest on top of the hill. There is no one near us. It is a little house in the forest. We have a paved road that was just loose gravel that kept clotted because the county coated it with tar at the end of every summer. Bits of gravel come from the surface of the road all the time. The gravel is loose on the steep banks for the road as it turns up and down the hillside. It is on a rounded path above the forest floor. If you go off the ditch, you will go down a steep slope into the trees. A few other people live out here with us. Old ladies keep rose gardens and sometimes goats in the side yard of their tiny houses. A farmhouse with a cattle field ringed by dense stands of old forest occupies the gentler slope above our house.

Mom is convinced the forest is dangerous. Black bears with sleek and iridescent fur like a bed of fly wings crawl up from their tunnels. Coyotes make their way down from the top of the hill to find chickens that stray from their coops. Hobos wearing worn blue jeans, torn plaid shirts, and muck encrusted sneakers wander from the other side of the valley where the Milwaukee Line went over the pass. They leave fire pits with blackened Bush's Best Baked Beans cans. Yet the forest is mostly empty except for the occasional old woman hunting for mushrooms.

I leave the house and Mom admonishes me not to go that far into the forest. I thought we had worked this out. "Where could I go? You know I won't go far. Just don't call me again or I may get stung by nettles. I have a watch. I'll be back in two hours."

"Is your watch wound?"

"Yes. Yes."

"Where are you going?"

"I don't know," I say. "I'm going into the forest."

"Don't get lost."

"I can't get lost. I've tried."

"Don't go far."

"Do you want to come with me?"

"Just say within earshot."

She wants me to carry her voice into the forest with me. I want to get away from her voice. When she says stay close, I want to go far. When she says don't get lost, I don't want to know where I am. I'd recovered from the nettles. I wear a loose secondhand t-shirt my father had been wearing. It only remembers my father riding on his Honda motorcycle until something happened to the bike that caused my father to start yelling and then he hung the bike from the rafters in the woodshed and now I have this t-shirt that remembers what it was like to ride on that Honda.

I want to see the sun. Under the cedar trees, I can hardly see in front of my hand. In the gloom, the trunks stand out and fall away into the darkness. There are the old ladies in the forest who collect mushrooms. I told my mother about them. Mom said be careful around strangers. The old ladies didn't seem like strangers even though I didn't know them. What do you call the people who were here before you were here? The forest was more familiar to them. I was the new one. Mom said, "Don't take anything they offer you. Don't take it especially if it's really good. I will get you something nice instead. Just tell me what it was, and I will get you something twice as nice." The old ladies will offer me toffees wrapped in wax paper and muffins folded into foil. I will tell my mother this, but I will also take the toffee and the muffins, and that way one toffee offered by a strange old lady in the forest will get transformed into three toffees in total. A lie is bad. Yet truth is unproductive. A half-lie, half-truth is fruitful. As I take the toffee from the old ladies, I say, "I can't. My Mom won't let me."

When I come home, I tell Mom what had happened up to my eating the toffee. "An old lady in the forest offered me a toffee," I say.

Mom scoffs. "Just now in the forest? She offered you candy?"

"Yes, it was wrapped in wax paper like she had made it herself."

"That could be really dangerous. It might not be toffee at all."

"It looked really good," I say. I want to tell her it tastes like cream and butter and salt, and I want more of them as soon as I have it. There is no way the store would have something as soft and flavorful and fresh as that toffee. Instead, the store is likely to have something as hard as an old Lego.

"I would have to go the store to get toffee," Mom says. She is under her afghan, and I can tell it will be a difficult act for her to get up and get a Tab from the fridge, much less go to the store. "You can have some baker's chocolate."

There is a square of semisweet chocolate in the cupboard that tasted and broke apart on my teeth just like an old crayon from the bottom of the toybox.

"You come back home as soon as you see those old ladies again," Mom says. "I don't like it that they are out there. What are they doing following you around in the forest?"

"I think they are collecting mushrooms," I say.

"Like hippies?"

"I don't know, Mom." After that the old ladies give me a muffin.

An old lady carrying a basket with chanterelles and goat's beard comes out of the bushes. She walks around the cedar trees and says to me, "This is good ground, dearie. Do you want a muffin?"

"My mom—"

"I don't see your mother here. You can have the muffin. It's nice. Everyone deserves a nice treat, don't they? No charge."

I can't help myself when presented with this logic. My mother isn't there. And I can get two more muffins with the story of the muffin. Mom doesn't need to know I have eaten the muffin. The muffin is moist and stuffed with seeds that I pick out from the crumble. The seeds crawl away, and one flutters up into the forest gloom. They are little beetles.

"It's all right," the old lady says, "They are edible. They don't mind being eaten."

"Alive! Eaten alive," I say. "They are alive."

"If you don't like them you don't have to swallow them. Some people don't seem to care for them very much."

"Where did they come from?"

"Mother's old recipe," the old lady says. "They add a bit of pizazz. But if you eat them, they will make your drowsy."

The crunch of the beetles remains with me, and I want another muffin, and I am pretty sure the store doesn't have muffins like the ones the old ladies had in the forest.

My mother makes me hot dogs and macaroni and cheese. It isn't grandma's recipe but something Mom concocted on her own while standing on the aisle of the Associated Grocers under the florescent light, one foot on a lime green Lino tile and the other foot on a white tile. I begged her at the time to get me a 24-ounce Coke can. It was the size of two cokes in a single can. I didn't get the can, but she had the idea of macaroni and hot dogs. After we eat, we sit on the couch while I wait for Dad to come back from the horse ranch and then get ready to go to the diner to cook. We watch a program where men are dressed as plush animals. There is bright, silly music and the sound of a slide whistle. The men run into walls and then fall and kick the plush soles of their feet at the sky. I am in the house as carefully wrapped as the wedding china on top of the cupboard.

The next day when I leave looking for some muffins, Mom says, "Where are you going? Stay in range. Don't get lost."

"I won't get lost."

"Don't run into the nettles, okay?"

"One time!"

I want to get as far away from her voice as possible. I wander into the forest and find the footprints of the old ladies. There is a Mary Jane footprint right in a rodent hill under the trees. It is left by a shrew, mole, or vole or some burrowing animal. I follow the trail, broken fern fronds and more tracks. More tracks join them until I follow a trail winding through the fir, maple, and cedar trees. I come to a clearing at dusk. The old ladies gather under the purple sky in clumps, knitting with needles rather than crochet hooks. The needles seem major league, dangerous compared to the blunt hooks. They stand in groups and whisper to each other. One old lady cackles and says, "Oh my."

They see me and ask me to come out where they can put an eye on me.

"Does your mother know where you are, dearie? Do your folks even know?"

"Would you like a muffin?"

I do want a muffin, and not despite the beetles, but because of them. I eat one muffin after another. There are baskets of them. I nod off and then wake when the old ladies lower me in a large wicker basket into a cavernous clay well in the center of the field. The clay walls drip run off water. I can see holes in the wall drilled by voles. Is this the same as getting lost?

I stand up and they said, "You can rest."

I grab the earth rim of the hole and find a handful of sod and root that hold me as I pull myself up onto the field. The old ladies make a cooing noise. The one nearest me says, "I like it. Spunk."

I start to walk, and the old ladies follow in a mass behind me offering toffee and muffins. I burp and a beetle spirals out of my left nostril. The ladies can't move as quickly as I can on my young, supple legs. I'm unsure of where I am, but I am not lost. The ladies flock behind me, appearing and reappearing behind the trees.

I come to my house. My mother looks up from under her afghan. "It's dark. I was worried. I called for you hours ago."

"I know Mom. I'm home now."

Outside the old ladies gather and wait. In the morning they have gone back into the forest. And I'm unsure if I want to risk seeing them again, even though when I wake I want a muffin with the beetles that drift away into the forest gloom. I am as free as a moth suspended in the wind.

Kim Fu in conversation with Kailee Haong
Spring 2022

Kim Fu is the author of the story collection *Lesser Known Monsters* of the 21st Century. Fu's first novel, *For Today I Am a Boy*, won the Edmund White Award for Debut Fiction and was a finalist for the PEN/Hemingway Award. Her second novel, *The Lost Girls of Camp Forevermore*, was a finalist for the Washington State Book Awards. Fu's writing has appeared in *Granta*, the *Atlantic*, the *New York Times*, and *BOMB*. She lives in Seattle.

Kailee Haong is a writer with work published in *Split Lip*, *The Inlander*, and elsewhere, as well as a contributing editor for *Moss*. She holds an M.F.A. in Creative Writing from Eastern Washington University.

Haong

As with any story collection I come across, I'm always curious as to how an author decides to organize and order the stories. In your collection, did you immediately know the order in which you wanted them to appear? Was there any reasoning in starting with "Pre-Simulation Consultation XF007867" and ending with "Do You Remember Candy?" What, if anything, did you take into consideration when arranging the stories?

Fu

As I was writing the stories, I had a general sense of where they would fit into a collection. Certain stories felt like early ones, middle ones, late ones. Certain stories felt like they should be grouped together, that they were thematically in dialogue with each other. "Do You Remember Candy" wasn't the last story written, but when I hit upon its final image, of a mother watching her daughter through the window, I knew I wanted to end the book with it.

The exact order of the stories was heavily influenced by my editor at Tin House, Masie Cochran. It was her idea to open with "Pre-Simulation," which had never occurred to me, and now I can't imagine it any other way. Written entirely in dialogue, as a computer-transcribed conversation without speaker tags, it's the only story not written in conventional prose. It throws you into the mechanics of a speculative world and technology with no lead-up. She thought it was attention-grabbing, the right story to set the tone of the book and the expectations of readers. I think I thought you had to ease readers into weirdness, where she—correctly—thought you should draw in the right readers immediately. Like, "Hey! Weirdness over here!"

Haong

I love that thought—"Hey! Weirdness over here!"—because the stories are indeed strange, and so idiosyncratic and fun to read. Are there any particular stories, books, or authors that have influenced you as a writer? Maybe others that also delve into this totally cool weirdness?

Fu

Absolutely! I recently did an event with Zach Powers, who described writers who work in the uncanny and fantastical as "team weird." For me, team weird includes Karen Russell, Kevin Brockmeier, and George Saunders, but also writers who infuse a sense of strangeness and magic into seemingly realist stories, like Heather O'Neill or Elizabeth McCracken. Ted Chiang's books were a huge influence on *Monsters*, as were Wicked Wonders by Ellen Klages, *Friday Black* by Nana Kwame Adjei-Brenyah, *Future Home of the Living God* by Louise Erdrich, *In the House Upon the Dirt Between the Lake and the Woods* by Matt Bell, and *The Vegetarian* by Han Kang. I just finished *Bitter Orange* by Claire Fuller, and the simmering unease and slow-building gothic horror were extremely inspiring to me, a feeling I want to evoke in my own writing.

Haong

Perhaps one of my favorite things about speculative fiction is this ability to write in a place that feels both futuristic and far-off, yet also so close and attainable in a scary-realistic way, as if tomorrow we could very well wake up, connect with an operator, and begin our first simulation. How do you walk this fine line of reality and unreality in your writing? I'm thinking also of books like *1984* and *Parable of the Sower*, now past or nearly past their settings, and how our world has conformed to some of those shapes and ideologies put into place in these novels, or bent in different ways. If we revisit *Lesser Known Monsters of the 21st Century* in a decade, will the concepts you've dreamt up feel even closer to reality?

Fu

A decade? I wonder that about tomorrow, or next week. For me, one of the challenges of writing speculative fiction is that technology outpaces the speed I can write, let alone publish. Actual technologies, but also just whatever nonsense comes out of the mouth of Elon Musk or Mark Zuckerberg. Last fall, I wrote 20,000 words of a novel that I ended up throwing away, because what was actually happening with Meta and NFTs and Web3 was more ridiculous and surreal than anything I could invent. I hope that focusing on the smaller, more human stories within these worlds will make something within them more timeless, regardless of how history unfolds. I recently read Erin Swan's debut, *Walk the Vanished Earth*, which is both speculative and a bit of an alt-history, a family lineage from a frontiersman in 1873 to a post-human creature on the moon in 2073, centered on an apocalyptic flood in 2018. Obviously, in our reality, Earth wasn't submerged in 2018, but the book nevertheless speaks to my own feelings about human ambition and frailty, my own fears and dreams.

Haong

Place is so influential in most authors' workers, whether obviously, by establishing cities, landmarks, or other blatant geographical mentions, or in more subtle ways, like describing dense forestry, towering mountain ranges, or, like in "Bridezilla," the small mentions of "wildfire smoke," "waterfront homes," and the "harbor cruise." How does the Northwest play a role in your writing? You've lived in different places in the Northwest, including Canada. Do you feel a stronger pull toward any specific place in your writings?

Fu

I love that you noticed those details. I grew up in Vancouver, BC and have lived in Seattle for over ten years; the Pacific Northwest is my home and permeates my writing. Superficially, the stories in Monsters are mostly set in nonspecific every-towns, but you're right, they're backgrounded by the mountains and the sea, moody grays and greens, ancient trees and ash on the wind. My previous novel, *The Lost Girls of Camp Forevermore*, was explicitly set along the West Coast, from BC to southern California. I sometimes think I'm drawn to a dream-version of the region, the way it feels as opposed to its literal geography. I find myself resistant to name, say, a Seattle street or landmark in a story, even as a local reader would recognize it in the details, the people, the energy.

Haong

You do a great job of conjuring this dream-version of the Northwest throughout your writings, even if place isn't something that's specifically called out or named, as you say. There's something so special about existing here, surrounded by the beauty of the region. Do you think you could imagine setting any future work in other places, or is there something about it here that will always be where your stories, essays, and poems call home?

Fu

Even as the Northwest has dominated my imagination, and I expect that will continue, other places and settings feature in my work as well. The story "June Bugs," about a house infested by a surreal volume of insects, was partially inspired by a residency I did in a small town in Saskatchewan. I'm grateful that my literary career has taken me to South Africa and a subarctic town in the Yukon and all over America, and that it all feeds into the well from which my worlds and details are drawn. That said, I find it hard to predict anything about what I write in the future. My interests as a writer are constantly shifting and changing in a way that feels outside of my control. I'm pretty sure my next book is set in the Pacific Northwest, but if it ends up being partially in New York City or on Mars by the time it's done, I wouldn't be that surprised.

Haong

Many of your stories in *Lesser Known Monsters of the 21st Century* touch on death or the notion of death as an ending, both metaphorical and literal. I'm also interested in how this "death as an ending" concept is subverted, specifically in "Twenty Hours," where death also marks a beginning. Could you talk about your relationship to death in writing? Do you find it more of an ending, a beginning, or maybe a mix of both?

Fu

People keep asking me about this! I think death is a preoccupation in my writing because it's such a huge part of human experience, yet—at least in my experience of North American culture—we talk about it so little. We *avoid* talking about it, thinking about it, preparing ourselves and each other for it. All that suppression makes it bubble up in the writerly subconscious. I don't think of death as just an ending, but a defining feature of life as we're living it: grief for those we've lost, the everyday knowledge of its inevitability.

Haong

You're absolutely right, death is so taboo. I recall losing my grandpa at a young age and the very respected, traditional Buddhist Chinese funeral processes that felt so natural to me growing up with immigrant grandparents, that maybe even desensitized me to death in a way that some cultures don't quite do (like rituals, open-casket viewings, offerings and incense at gravesites, etc.). In that case, for me, growing up, it was so talked about that it felt normal. Will you continue talking (and writing) about death?

Fu

Yes, because it feels so fundamental to me. I wouldn't know how to write the story of any life without it being touched by death—literal deaths, but also the fear of death, the desire for death, the beliefs around it, the question of legacy and what remains.

My parents were also Chinese immigrants, but I had very a different experience from what you describe. I felt disconnected from those rites when I was a child; my mother is a Baptist Christian, and traditional Chinese offerings and rituals were a site of confusion and contention. When my father passed away, I felt protective of my family's privacy and his dignity, unwilling to talk about the most formative and painful experience of my life. I also quickly felt a lot of pressure from the outside world to pretend that I was okay, that I'd gotten over it, when I'm not sure I ever will. Fiction and poetry have felt like a safe space to explore those feelings more obliquely.

Haong

How do the current events of today play a role in your writing? I hate to bring up anything pandemic-related, but I couldn't help but compare the loss of taste and the pleasure of eating in "Do You Remember Candy" to the very real situation many people have faced after COVID has drastically limited their abilities to taste and smell. Do you consider the things occurring in our world today in your writings, or are your stories, poems, and novels a way to escape those things, and to create worlds of your own?

Fu

I wrote "Do You Remember Candy" in 2019, and while editing the book in 2020 and 2021, I was really worried that it would come across as offensive or painful in a way I didn't intend. I've since heard from a few readers who did lose their sense of smell or taste to COVID, who felt the story took their pain seriously in a way they hadn't encountered before. I hope that's how the story comes across in general.

This speaks to your previous question, too—why I write about death so much. I think most writers write about what's happening in the world today whether we want to or not. Even if I were trying to write the most fantastical, escapist scenario, I live in this world, in the present moment, and so does the reader. The reader and I will both bring to the story our own experiences, our anxieties, our worldviews. The metaphors and parallels will be unavoidable. I think it's important, while writing and especially while editing, to consider and hone those interpretations, rather than deny them.

Haong

I want to linger on the idea of both you and the reader bringing experiences, anxieties, and worldviews to whatever story is at hand. What do you hope readers might walk away with after reading *Lesser Known Monsters of the 21st Century*, or any of your other work, for that matter?

Fu

While I think there are some obvious themes and satirical jabs in *Monsters*—for example, I think you can tell I'm both awed and disturbed by human resilience, how we can seemingly adapt to and come to accept anything—there isn't any one big takeaway. I mostly hope readers leave feeling entertained, engaged, unsettled, provoked, full of their own new thoughts and ideas. Part of taking the reader's experience into account is knowing that a work of fiction, while it's being read, is a construction in their mind, and leaving space for that kind of collaboration. I love hearing from readers about their own interpretations and connections to the stories.

Haong

I'd love to hear a little about your writing process in general. How do you get into your groove to create these fantastical worlds that are so fun to exist in while reading?

Fu

I can't start writing without a sensory detail, something I can see, smell, feel, taste, or touch. If an idea comes to me another way—as a scenario, a what-if, a type of person, an invention, a scrap of dialogue—it won't go anywhere until I can find an image to let me in. My first drafts are an intuitive and messy process, not knowing where I'm going or what happens next, stacking images and seemingly unrelated scraps together, experimenting, writing non-linearly, writing whatever piece interests me in the moment. That draft just lets me see what the story even is, and then I start over again. I don't plan or outline before I begin; if I outline, it'll be between draft one and two. I throw away a lot of first drafts that don't have that energy, where there isn't something that draws me back, that makes me want to revisit the world and make it work. I won't pretend this is an efficient way to write, but it's the only way that works for me.

Haong

You're a very busy writer, balancing book-related events and teaching—what's the secret to carving out time to write or be creative?

Fu

I work best around other people, especially when I'm first starting something new, or when I'm feeling stuck or burned out. While I was writing *Monsters*, I was fortunate to receive a couple artist residencies, and I cultivated friendships with other writers who could meet up in coffee shops or each other's homes, and I also went to writing groups that I found online, including one that met in the basement of the library. It's easy to feel like writing new work isn't as important as other gigs, as you mention, which have more immediate deadlines or paychecks. I love the energy of being with other people who are also choosing to carve out this time, who are taking their writing seriously, even for an hour or two. We don't have to share work or even know each other. Just by showing up, we're holding each other accountable. I get so much just from listening to their keyboards clack or their pens scritch across the page.

Haong

You are one of those do-it-all type of writers that I absolutely aspire to be someday, dabbling in just about every form of writing out there. Do you feel particularly called toward any one in particular—fiction, nonfiction, poetry, or do you find yourself filling those buckets equally? How would you say your style and subject matter tend to differ when writing in different genres?

Fu

As I mentioned, my writerly interests seem to be constantly changing in ways I can't predict. When I was doing interviews for my first novel, back in 2014, I self-described as primarily a poet. While I was promoting my poetry collection in 2016, I was working on a lot of essays and reported nonfiction. As I finished my second novel and started working on *Monsters*, I was thoroughly and exclusively obsessed with short stories. I wrote nothing else, and nothing else interested me. Right now, my attention is turning back to the novel, to its expansive possibilities, the slow layering of meaning, the long journeys to which I haven't had access while working in shorter forms.

Haong

Are there any works-in-process we can look forward to reading in the future?

Fu

I'm working on a new novel. It's in an extremely early phase, where even the basic premise is in flux. When people ask me what it's about, my answer changes week to week. I'm still just playing with the characters, generating a lot of material that will probably all end up in the trash, letting it find its shape.

Kids playing in Cottage Lake, 1964.
City Light Negatives (Record Series 1204-01), Seattle Municipal Archives.

#ClimbingNation
From *Lesser Known Monsters of the 21st Century*
Kim Fu

As April came in the door, she could immediately tell that the two magnetic poles of Travis's memorial were his older sister, Miki, and his climbing partner, Zach. Everyone gathered around one or the other. April recognized them both from Travis's Instagram. Miki sat with her feet up on the sofa in the living room that backed into the foyer, where she could both talk to the people sprawled at her feet on the rug and greet newcomers as they came through the front door, without getting up. She nodded at April as though they knew each other. Miki wore a black bodysuit and a patterned scarf the size of a beach blanket. The scarf was a riot of colors, and she held an end in each hand, so the fabric moved and fluttered around her as she gestured. Miki had a straight up-and-down body and long, elegant hands, amber eyes, and a triangular heap of curls that fell halfway down her back. She was appealing to look at, like a glazed cake.

Zach presided over the small kitchen, on the opposite end of the open-plan main floor. Casserole dishes and bottles of wine gathered on the counters. Zach wore gray technical shorts with oversized pockets and a plaid button-down, the sleeves rolled up and only the center two buttons done, so the tails flared out at the bottom and golden chest hair glinted over the top. He wasn't dressed appropriately, but who could blame him?

Leaning back against the sink, he was appealing to look at in precisely the same way.

April beelined for the end of what amounted to a receiving line to talk to Zach. She found herself smiling, or grimacing, her mouth upturned involuntarily. "How awful," everyone said. "What a thing to witness. You must be a wreck. I'm so sorry. If you want to talk, I'm here." Their faces locked in those same smile-grimaces, as they patted him on the shoulder, the forearm. Lingering.

She looked out the window. The quiet street wound in wide curves, lined with trees, as in only the oldest, most expensive neighborhoods: cathedral-high elms touching canopy from opposite sides of the median, weeping beech sweeping their hair along the sidewalk, magnolias in full, pink bloom. Two teenage girls, standing at the end of the driveway, whispered in close conference, heads together, as though debating whether to go inside. They turned and stared back at April. She wondered if they'd also gotten the address from the obituary. Did teenagers even know about newspaper obituaries?

It was startling that the large room was filled with people her own age or younger, like a house party. She'd only been to funerals and memorials and wakes for elderly relatives—she had been lucky in that way. A bewildered widow or widower at the center, equally aged friends and siblings ringed tightly around them, oblivious small children running around the outside perimeter, April somewhere in between. Where, she wondered, were his parents, his aunts and uncles? When she pulled up outside, she'd assumed this house belonged to his parents; the two-story craftsman had an older, lived-in sensibility.

"I'm glad you weren't injured," the woman in front of April said, to Zach. "I mean, obviously I wish Travis had survived. I wish it hadn't happened at all! And of course it's the worst thing that could happen to a person, to you. I mean, not as bad as what happened to Travis. I mean, I'm just glad that you're physically—"

"I know what you meant," Zach said. "Thank you." He clasped her hand between both of his. As soon as he released his grip, she turned and fled from the room.

April knew it was an unfair thought, but up close, Zach did not look grief-stricken, like a haunted survivor. He had a healthy, well-rested glow. "I'm April," she said, stepping forward. "Travis and I were friends in college. I'm so sorry for your loss."

Zach studied her, and she felt caught in the lie. She and Travis had gone to the same college and lived in the same dorm building. In theory, they'd gone to the same parties, stood in the same rooms, but she couldn't remember if they'd ever actually met.

A few months earlier, he'd seemingly popped up on all her social media feeds at once: a tiny figure in an endless series of high-altitude landscapes, snowy fields above smokelike clouds, jagged cliffs piercing the sun. She'd been surprised to see that someone she'd plausibly known had five hundred thousand followers on Instagram, the population of a midsize city. She had no interest in mountaineering, yet she'd spent hours looking at close-ups of his knots, his blistered hands and shredded knuckles, his gear knolled on flat rocks. She'd watched hundreds of short videos of him leaping for a hold or pulling himself up a chimney, clicked "like" on hundreds of pictures of him posed hanging from a wall, or standing backlit and triumphant at the peak. One point four million thumbs up for his hypnotic charisma in a YouTube video. She gathered that he had only recently become popular, that everyone had found him at almost the same moment she did. The algorithm, mysterious as fate. He was less a person than a quilt of these beautifully colored squares. His view of the world from above, geographic and breathtaking, was so different from wherever she was: squatting over the toilet in her dark bathroom, lying in bed with a bag of unsalted tortilla chips balanced on her chest. He'd had the aura of a celebrity, and his sudden, violent death, his appearance in the mainstream news, felt perversely fitting. The famous should die famously.

"Thank you," Zach said.

"Can I ask . . ." April paused. "I understand if you don't want to talk about it, but I only know what I read in the news." She tried to soften her tone. "How did it happen?"

The news stories had been brief but vivid. Zach and Travis had been on a day climb in the North Cascades. A storm came in, and they wanted to get down quickly to avoid it. Something went wrong. Travis fell three hundred feet. The longest article that April had seen was padded out by embedded social media posts. Travis's last post, a selfie in the car with Zach, mugging with their tongues out, #climbingnation, flooded with comments and crying emojis. April added one that felt true enough—"I still can't believe it. You were an inspiration."—and felt a little thrill to see it pop up in the article, gathering hearts.

The room went silent. Miki craned her long neck in their direction.

Zach shook his head, his bangs falling into his eyes. He combed them back with his fingers. "It wasn't even forecasted to rain," he said. "It happened really fast. The wind picked up, the sky went dark. We knew we had to bail. We decided to do a simul-rappel. It's an emergency maneuver to get down fast, where you rappel down at the same time, using each other as a counterbalance."

Zach lifted his gaze. A rapt audience surrounded him. April noticed the teenage girls had come inside, hovering just past the threshold in the foyer. "One mistake, man. Travis made one mistake. The rope slipped through, and there was nothing I could do. He was just gone."

April could see it from Zach's perspective: the rocks darkened and slick in the rain. His muscles trembling with exhaustion as he held his body tight to the wall. A sudden, sickening loss of tension. Watching Travis fall, the loose coil of rope falling after him. Zach reaching out a futile hand, his scream drowned out in a roll of thunder. A lightning flash illuminating nothing, Travis too far below to see.

"And then what?"

April turned to the voice. Sitting in an armchair at Miki's side, the man who'd spoken looked like he'd come from the same mold as Zach and

Travis: about the same age, with the same wiry build, deep tan, and shaggy hair. He wore a black suit over a T-shirt with no tie. "How did you get down and back to the car?" he said.

"I didn't," Zach said. "I waited on a ledge for help."

"You both fell, but there was a ledge on your side?"

"I didn't fall. I climbed down to the ledge."

"You were on the ledge when Travis fell? Like you'd gotten to the ledge first?"

"No, I climbed down to the ledge after Travis fell."

"Did the anchor fail?"

"Obviously not," Zach snapped. "I already said that he . . ."

He wiped at his eyes. "You know what, Nick? I don't want to talk about this anymore."

April stepped closer to Zach. She rubbed him gently on the back. "At least Travis was doing something he loved," she said.

"He was," Zach said, sounding grateful. "He really was."

Nick exchanged a look with Miki, who shook her head with a slight smile, as though they were agreeing to indulge Zach on this. Nick's dark suit was a little too large for him. He sat slouched on the chair with his knees wide apart, the fabric pooling around him like a shadow.

Someone opened the unscreened windows, and the suburban noises, alien to April, joined the low din of the room: a screeching child's laugh, a bird singing incongruously into the evening. The hush of plants nestling against each other in the wind. The absence of cars. Miki turned on a floor lamp, still without getting up, and the circle of light around her seemed to grow brighter and more defined as it won its war of attrition against the sun.

The casseroles cooled and hardened. The wine bottles were emptied. When only a handful of people remained, April took it upon herself to start refilling everyone's glasses, opening a new bottle each time one was drained. The bottle opener was in the first drawer she tried, and she moved around the kitchen confidently, as though she knew it well.

She bent at the waist and reached diagonally across Zach's chest to pour red into his glass, her chest close to his chin where he sat. "April, you said, right? I don't think Travis ever mentioned you. You guys were close, back in the day?"

"You know how it is," she said. "We saw each other every day when we were in school, and then we fell out of touch. I always meant to reconnect. And then I missed my chance." She held the bottle against her body. Her eyes stung. How sad that would be, if it were true.

"Wow," he said. "To be honest, I was surprised there were so many people here. Travis was kind of a secretive guy, hard to get close to. I always thought he didn't have that many friends."

"Secretive?" April said. "He had half a million Instagram followers."

"Well, he was a climber and a photographer. That's not, like, actually knowing someone."

"He was secretive," Miki chimed in. Her voice was musical, regionless, and her mouth opened wide when she talked. April had once clicked through a tagged photo—@mikimikimiki, #siblinggoals—and seen, under her name and profile picture, the words Theater Artist. She waved at a group of people who were murmuring parting condolences as they left. One patted Miki on the shoulder awkwardly as he passed. Now April was alone with Miki, Zach, and Nick.

"He had a lot of strange ideas," Miki said, "but he knew he had to keep them to himself for the sake of his internet presence, business, whatever it was." She gestured with her empty wineglass. April sidled over with the bottle, pleased to be useful in this way, to blend in like the help. "Thank you, April."

"I did feel like he kept me at a distance," Zach said. "We'd drive and camp for days and days, but we mostly talked logistics and online shit."

"You put your lives in each other's hands," Miki said. "I can't imagine anything more intimate."

"That's just climbing. Sometimes you do that with people you just met." Zach shifted in his seat.

"You fuck people you just met, but if you keep fucking them, it becomes intimate all the same."

April put the bottle on the coffee table and slid in beside Miki on the couch, Nick on Miki's other side. "What kind of strange ideas?"

Miki twirled her scarf. "What was that?"

"You said Travis had a lot of strange ideas that he kept from his internet fans."

"Oh, you know, he was one of those people who thought the world was ending. Not in the biblical, street-preacher way. Climate change, peak oil. Global pandemic. That sort of thing."

"That's not so strange," Nick said. "Doesn't everyone feel that way by now?"

"But I could see how that wouldn't go with his internet persona," April said. Travis's blandly inspirational captions, the royalty-free rock music to which he set his videos, the continuous summits, peaks without valleys, had lately been the best diversion from the apocalyptic news.

"For Travis it went beyond that. He was prepared. Preparing." She looked around, meeting each of their eyes in turn.

Miki's thick, black eyebrows and eyelashes made her eyes burn a lighter brown, almost gold. She shrugged exaggeratedly and the wine sloshed in her glass. "I guess I can tell you all. It doesn't matter now."

She settled into the couch in a way that made her seem larger than before, her arms open, her chest expanded, the scarf pulled outward to either side. In the silence, April became aware that sometime in the last few minutes, the sun had dropped below the hard line of the horizon. All at once, it was night, the open windows portals to a depthless blue, the closed windows watery mirrors.

"He had a cabin," Miki said. "Not that far east along Highway Two, but deep in the bush, in the mountains. It was impossible to get to, on purpose. No roads. Days of bushwhacking, scrambling, free-climbing, river crossings. Completely inaccessible in the winter. High altitude. Functionally a fortress, surrounded by danger. I knew about it, but only he knew where it was. That is, until he died, and I got the deed to the land."

"Have you been?" April asked.

"I only just got the papers. And how would I get there? I could look into chartering a helicopter, I suppose, assuming there's somewhere to land."

"I find it hard to believe there's anywhere like that in the state that isn't either parkland or part of a reserve," Nick said.

"Believe what you like," Miki said. "That's how Travis described it, and I believe him. That's why he chose to build the cabin there."

"How did he even find the plot to buy in the first place?" Nick asked.

"I don't know," Miki said. She smoothed out a spot on her thigh where her bodysuit had ridden up and wrinkled. "I don't know, because when he told me about it, I was furious."

"Why?" April asked.

"Well, what does it say about who he planned to spend the end of the world with? Certainly not me. I'd never make it. Either he meant to go it alone, or . . ." Miki gestured at Nick and then Zach. "Or with his adventuring buddies."

"He never mentioned it to us," Zach said, quietly.

Nick continued to press. "If it's so hard to access, how did he construct the cabin? How did he get the materials and tradespeople there?"

"According to the documents, it's more like a shack," Miki said. "And he built it himself. As for how he got the materials there, I would guess—piece by piece."

April pictured Travis free-climbing with a bundle of two-by-fours strapped to his back. That part, if nothing else, fit into his internet aesthetic.

"I suppose I will have to go eventually," Miki went on. "It'd be a shame to let all the supplies go to waste."

"He was already keeping it stocked?" April asked.

Miki nodded. "He could only schlep so much in at one time, but I think at this point there's quite a lot of shelf-stable food, fuel, and water. And he was installing a gravity pump, I remember."

"There was a water source even higher up than the cabin?" Nick said.

Miki waved one end of the scarf. "Nick, I only know what Travis told me. I only learned where this place even is in the last couple days."

"I'm amazed you got the deed already," April said. "When my great-aunt died, the bureaucracy of it all took forever."

"Travis had a will," Miki said. "He'd update it before he went on any big adventure trip, particularly overseas. Ironic that he died on a day climb practically in his backyard." Throughout the conversation, Miki's tone had been droll, almost amused, dry of grief. She stared into the middle distance. "Maybe I'll let the place rot up there. In a thousand years, an archaeologist can puzzle over it, all the gold."

"Gold?" they chorused.

Miki laughed. "I told you, he was one of those people. He thought only gold would be worth anything in the new world order. I know he was regularly buying one-ounce bars from a place on the Eastside and stashing them in the cabin."

Nick was already looking it up on his phone. "Right now, an ounce of gold is worth about twelve hundred dollars."

Miki's features were large, cartoonishly expressive. She could lift her eyebrows almost to her hairline. "Good Lord. Well, no wonder he had almost nothing in the bank." She stretched in her seat. "I guess I will have to go to the cabin after all. That's too much money to leave for future archaeologists."

Nick shook his head. "This just doesn't sound like Travis to me. He was the most optimistic person I knew."

"There's optimism in being prepared," Miki said.

"And I thought he was a big believer in never even hiking alone. Safety in numbers and all that. I can't imagine him bushwhacking, solo, to his fortress of gold."

"Death," Miki began, seemingly pausing for effect, "has a way of unveiling the truth. But as you said, Travis was many things. Let's talk about some of the others. April, I would love to hear what he was like in college."

"Oh." April put her glass on the table and topped it up. "Nick, Zach, did you guys know him then?"

Zach shook his head. He hadn't spoken in a while, and his expression was distant, faintly disturbed. "We met after, when we were all working at the same ski resort."

"How about you, Miki? Were you in close contact?"

"No, not really. Travis and I were close growing up, and later when I moved back, right up until he died." Miki's voice continued to strike April as strange, overenunciated, with a perpetual note of irony. "But we lost touch a bit when he was in college. I was living in LA, and my life was busy, and not terribly pleasant." April sipped her wine and considered. "Everybody loved him," she said, finally. "He was funny, and he had a way of addressing a room full of people and making it feel like he was only talking to you. Girls would leave little Post-it Notes on his dorm room door." She was thinking of his vlogs and their comment sections.

Miki seemed to waver for the first time. She laughed again, softer, more bitterly. "That sounds right."

April wasn't sure when she'd fallen asleep, but she woke up and Nick and Miki were also out, the three of them huddled together on the couch. Zach wasn't in the room. April padded down the hall, her dry lips crusted violet from the wine, looking for a bathroom.

Coming around the corner, she could see into a study through the glass panels of its French doors. The lamp on the desk was on, its head downcast, blasting the tabletop with a startlingly bright, yellow light in the otherwise dark room. She heard the artificial shutter sound of a phone camera. It took her a moment to see Zach bent over the desk, taking photos of the papers arranged there.

The bathroom was before the study, along the same wall. She ducked in to use it, and then rejoined the others in the living room. Zach had not returned. She curled back up against Miki, who stirred but didn't wake.

Zach came back in a few minutes later. He gently shook Miki by the arm. "Miki? I'm going to go."

She grabbed on to his wrist without opening her eyes. "Let's stay in touch, okay?"

"Of course."

Nick wasn't fully awake until the front door had opened and closed. "Did Zach leave?"

Miki made a noise of assent.

Nick exhaled a long breath. "I feel bad for him. I really do. It's the kind of mistake anyone could make, and to be responsible for your best friend's death . . . That's devastating. Unbelievably devastating. But his denial is fucked up."

Miki removed her scarf, which she had been using as a blanket, and draped it over the top of the couch. It had become a part of her body in April's mind. It was like watching Miki pop her arm from its socket, or strip off her skin. Though the bodysuit went almost to her ankles, the material was thin and stretched to translucence. "It doesn't matter. Travis is gone either way."

"It doesn't bother you? Having him blame Travis?"

Miki started gathering up the glasses. April rose to help her. "Whatever he has to tell himself to get through, I understand."

"How do you know he's lying?" April said.

Nick looked at Miki, who nodded. "There aren't that many ways that only one person falls from a simul-rap," he said. "Zach must have lost control of the brake and not tied an end-stop knot. It sounds to me like he got to a ledge and just unweighted without thinking—took his weight off the rope—as you usually do when you touch ground rappelling. So the rope slid through his device, there was no time to grab it, no knot at the end . . ." Nick rubbed his face. His cheeks were flushed from the alcohol and creased from sleep. "I'm just speculating, but I can't think of a way

Travis could have made a mistake that led to his own fall in that setup. If Travis had fucked up, either they both would have fallen, or just Zach."

Miki and April put the glasses by the sink. Without asking, April put the stopper in the drain and started to fill one basin with hot water and soap.

"I wish I could be as understanding as you, Miki," Nick said. "I can barely look at him." He ran a hand through his floppy bangs, the same gesture Zach had made earlier, through the same haircut. April had seen Travis do the same thing while speaking directly to the camera held in his other hand. "I know it was an accident, but I blame him. It's his fault that Travis is gone. I want to grab him and shake him and ask how he could forget to tie a fucking knot. It'd be easier if he just admitted it. I think I could forgive him then. But now, now it feels . . ." Nick's voice cracked.

Miki left April to wash the glasses. She came and folded Nick into her arms. She was only a hair taller than him, but her long limbs and the way he shrank and crumbled in the embrace made them resemble a mother and child. "Nick," she said, speaking into his hair, "why don't you go home and go to sleep? We're all going to be dealing with this for a long time. One day at a time, okay?"

Nick nodded. He swiped at his eyes as he and Miki pulled apart. He paused at the front door in his rumpled suit and said, "It was nice to meet you, April. I wish it could have been under better circumstances."

April nodded, unable to speak. The door clicked shut.

Miki walked the perimeter of the room, turning on all the lights, closing the windows, lowering the blinds. April set the wineglasses in the rack to dry and started rooting around in the drawers for plastic wrap to cover the mummified casseroles. "It's so kind of you to stay and clean up when no one else did," Miki said. "Leaving me to grieve in a messy house. Some friends."

"I have to tell you something."

"Oh?"

"I saw Zach, earlier. While you were asleep. In the study. Taking pictures of some papers with his phone. I'm going to guess they were related to the cabin."

Miki turned and tugged on the cord to lower the last set of blinds. She was silent for a long moment. Finally, she said, "Did you notice those two teenage girls today?"

"What? Did you hear what I said about Zach?"

"The girls arrived at about the same time you did. When I asked them who they were, they admitted they were just fans of Travis online. They'd never met him. At first, I was going to ask them to leave, but then I thought, who was I to say they didn't know him just as well as any of us? Zach didn't know Travis enough to say whether or not he was a doomsday prepper. And Zach was the one who got him killed."

April put down the box of plastic wrap. Her gaze darted to the front door.

"Strangers loved my brother, and I have hundreds—thousands—of pictures and videos to remember him by. That's kind of beautiful, in its way." Miki was still staring at the covered window, the dusty vinyl an inch from her face. "It's a crazy story, isn't it?"

"How Travis died?"

"No. Well, that too. But I meant the cabin. A hidden trove of gold, where only the most skilled mountaineer can reach it! A treasure map left in plain sight, when you can just download templates for wills and deeds off the internet. It's like something out of a children's book. Knowing Zach, he probably started packing a gear bag the second he got home, not wanting me and my helicopter to beat him." Miki laughed. "Nick was driving me nuts with all those questions. 'How did Travis find it? How did he build? How could a place like that exist in this state?'"

The wine felt like a dying animal in April's gut, and the embedded ceiling lights Miki had turned on were queasily bright. April edged out of the kitchen, toward Miki and the door beyond. She was only just beginning to understand. "Does it?"

"Of course. There's plenty of high, remote places, that would take days or weeks of backpacking to get to, surrounded by terrain that could easily maim or kill you in the approach. Especially if you were expecting a big cache of supplies and water when you got there." Miki finally turned.

Pinprick reflections in her eyes glittered like stars. "Are you leaving?" she asked abruptly, seeing April standing in the middle of the room.

"I . . . Yes. I'm sorry again for your loss."

Miki showed her teeth, her mouth twisted to the side, somewhere between a grin and a sneer. "Didn't you lose him too?"

Miki stayed where she was, leaving April to see herself out. She didn't have a coat. April closed the door behind her. She hadn't realized she'd been holding her breath until she let it out on their front stoop, suddenly gulping air. This neighborhood had fewer streetlights than hers, and besides the one she'd just left, all of the houses were dark. Zach and Nick were long gone, no sign of anyone on the sidewalk.

In her car, she took out her phone. Her battery was almost dead. All of Travis's accounts had been deleted or changed to private, sometime that day, a large error block in the news articles where the embedded posts had been. As had Miki's. Without them, she couldn't think of a way to connect to Zach. His last name, in the articles, was uselessly common, and she couldn't remember his handles. She did not, in fact, know these people at all. She imagined trying to explain this to the police, that Zach might die trying to steal something that didn't exist. She didn't know where Miki had sent him, where they should look. She imagined a skeptical officer sitting across from her, in the middle of the night, in the station for this sleepy, wealthy suburb. Middle-aged but still getting the graveyard shift, the skin of his face puffy and cracked like overrisen cake, someone peripherally aware of Instagram and YouTube as something his children did. And who are you, he'd ask. Who are you to them?

Machines
Keygan S. S. McClellan

I can already smell the misty breath of the Pacific and the twenty or so tons of rotting animal by the time the SUV bounces from pavement to wet sand. Gray sky, gray horizon, gray sea, gray whale. I smear perfume in a scarf and tie it around my face to block out the odor: a small mountain of decaying insides I know will soon be exposed, the pond of thick, dark blood.

I trudge out over damp sand, my rubber boots slapping. The body looms like an obelisk tipped on its side, just as holy and desecrated. She was a juvenile gray whale, *Eschrictius robustus*, found beached and dead near Grayland, Washington.

In death, she looks deflated. Collapsed. Tipped a little onto her left side, a deep pool of blood building around her head. White scarring dots and scrapes her pliant, thick skin. The team—stranding responders from Cascadia Research Collective, responders from the Washington Department of Fish and Wildlife, and representatives from the Westport Aquarium (they want her bones)—circle and flock vulture-like around the body. We set up a barrier of caution tape, unfold a plastic table to stash tissue samples and data sheets, set to work measuring and probing the whale's exterior.

I touch, with my boot then with gloved fingers, the rubbery, supple skin. The great flukes are like giant paddles, stiff, dotted with whale lice, as big around as my eyes, that the researchers collect during their measurements.

The first thing we notice after this circling is the head. Our main objective is to determine the whale's cause of death, and it becomes quickly apparent. The response coordinator for Cascadia, my direct supervisor here, stands over the whale's tilted face, outlining with her gloved hands the concavity above the brow. The whale's skull has been caved in: she was probably hit and killed by a ship.

The researchers carve into the thick skin and blubber, pulling it open to reveal the mess of organic inflammation above the eye. A sharp probe lets loose a spurt of bright green pus, pungent bacterial odor rising. They collect some, dig further, find the fractures in the skull, the signs of infection and swelling. She didn't die immediately.

I back away, move upwind, breathe.

During the harbor seal necropsy a few weeks ago, we discovered that the smell of blood (metallic, wet, cloying, heady) makes me feel faint, so after the initial inspection, they set me to record data, mostly tissue samples destined for various researchers and agencies. The others, meanwhile, cut giant slices in her sides, sawing into blubber a handspan thick to begin flensing, exposing her organs for sample collection. They sink meat hooks into the slices and yank, forcing with brute strength the layers to peel back, her insides to be outside.

The researchers warn each other to take care—the rot has likely built up gases inside the carcass, ready to erupt. They probe at the sacs surrounding her organs. Suddenly, a clot of intestine bursts from her belly, pale pink-gray and dewy in the dim, clouded light. Gas escapes her body with wet, rattling hisses. The work to collect tissue samples begins in earnest before the rot can degrade them further.

The smell overwhelms me for a moment; I go stand near the caution tape barrier to breathe again. Onlookers have been filtering in and out of my awareness all morning; this time I engage with them, explaining what's going on and what we're trying to do. Explaining it feels better than the actual act of the necropsy. I escape into the insubstantial spark of thoughts and voice, ignore the gory reality of the body.

But I can't escape the reality of the body.

On a field trip to the Olympic peninsula, a coastline of temperate rainforest and rocky tidepools, my marine science class stops at a tiny convenience store to rest and look for last-minute supplies. As usual, I browse the handful of aisles to examine packages of noodles, granola bars, organic snacks, always looking for something I can't quite place. My eyes just want to take it all in.

The instructor, Trisha, and some of my classmates start talking with the older couple at the counter. A lot of talking. An inexplicable connection blossoms between our groups, and they usher us into the backroom to share tea, snacks, and stories. Enchanted, I snag a few crackers to dip in hummus and listen.

Trisha tells them about our class: we're studying marine environments, writing hypothetical research proposals, planning how to communicate science to non-scientists. The couple tells us about their home, and somehow get into a story.

They woke up one night to strange sounds. Songs. Low calls from the bay. They headed to the shoreline, identifying the sounds as whales. Night drowned the air in silence and pale stars, illuminating slanting puffs of vapor as giants breathed just above the glistening water surface.

The two got in their boat, paddled carefully and quietly into deeper water.

The woman tells us how she felt some connection, then. She calls it a religious experience, deeply spiritual. She tells us she's always been able to feel when whales enter the bay.

They narrate how, that night, one of the gray whales bobbed up to the surface, tilted its face, and examined the couple with one enormous eye. She says she felt the presence of a conscious mind regarding her, interrogating.

Talk shifts to whales in general, how many cultures and individuals, like these small business owners from the rural Washington coast, have regarded them as almost divine beings. Gray whales are known for how they examine humans in particular ways. In the San Ignacio Lagoon in Baja California, humans and gray whales meet each other yearly. During the calving season, giant mothers bring their newborns to the surface, where visitors wait in inflatable boats to stroke barnacle-crusted skin, hard jaws, rubbery gums. The ritual continues annually with little explanation except connection. Biological bodies meet and commingle; we derive significance from these events, corporeal and organic as we are.

We leave the little store with a fount of well-wishes. I'm thinking about whales.

With a few exceptions, humans don't hunt whales anymore. But we do kill them. The violence comes from carelessness.

During my summer as an unpaid intern at Cascadia, research biologist and founder John Calambokidis and the intern coordinator Kiirsten Flynn taught me much about the organization's research on large whales in the Pacific. Large whales spend a lot of time near the surface of the water, moving slowly, leaving them vulnerable to getting hit by ships and boats. Indeed, many of the humpback whale flukes I saw during my sessions of organizing photos into Cascadia's database, wherein whales are identified on an individual level according to the unique colors and patterns on their tails or dorsal regions, were scarred by propeller marks.

Cascadia researchers frequently conduct projects involving the attachment of suction cup tracking tags to large whales. This, combined with photo identification, allows them to track individuals and populations. They also tag whales and monitor their responses and behavior around ships. During one project, they found that in the Santa Barbara Channel, California—a busy shipping lane for cargo vessels—ships hit and killed at least five blue whales in 2007.[1] Cascadia partnered with other organizations to research the problem, resulting in the Vessel Speed Reduction Program, which incentivizes ships to reduce their speed through the channel.

Along North America's Atlantic coastline, meanwhile, human industry threatens one whale species with extinction. Less than five hundred northern right whales survive, a tiny fragment of a population almost wiped out by whaling. In this decimated network, every life lost represents a tremendous blow. According to calculations of population viability, right whales can sustain only one death per year if they are to survive. But in the first half of 2019, for example, over 1 percent of the remaining population died—in total, six whales, including some of the less than one hundred breeding females left alive.[2] Before then, in 2018, NOAA researcher Peter Corkeron expressed a belief that "we can save them."[3] But major threats continue, including ship strikes and entanglements in crab and lobster trap lines. Propellers slice through bodies and sever spines. Bows crush skulls. Ropes dig through flesh. Unless we see the bodies, the collective doesn't notice. The ships chug on. New England's lobster and crab trapping continues. The machinery of industrial humankind threatens existence itself—millions of years of genetic legacy slammed and lacerated and cut from the world, and not even on purpose.

My daughter and I almost went the way of the stricken whales in 2015 on Interstate-94 as it diverges and loops south into I-494. It only took a moment of inattention, a moment of carelessness by the man who, in all other ways, has shown me utter care.

The rear of a gray SUV fills the sky all at once, a wall of fiberglass and lightweight alloys. Our red Ford crunches into the other vehicle at fifty miles per hour. I don't hear, don't see, and there is no pain, but I feel the impact. My body lurches against the seatbelt, yanked up and down by tremendous pressure.

My senses return when time again speeds up. Hot smell, acrid and smoky. The sound of my own voice, gasping. Pain low in my belly. My eyes focus on the deflated airbag, dingy, now taking up space that moments ago was empty.

He bursts out his own door on the driver side, takes a few tries to force open the passenger door, helps me to the side of the road. I assess myself: pain, functional limbs. It's hard to think over my panic. I'm five months pregnant, and feel hurt there. Really hurt.

He holds my body close, neither of us thinking to call anyone, just honed in on the small world between us, caught on a liminal edge. The future could suddenly be anything.

We hear sirens soon anyway. An off-duty first responder who witnessed the crash comes to my side to help me stay calm. I've never felt so helpless.

Everything after takes too long.

The ambulance ride and medical assessment take too long. I wait too long in the hospital hallway, feeling only waves of pain and fear. The ultrasound reassures me that my organs and my baby are okay for now. I wait longer for them to monitor us overnight.

Bed rest and the recovery from deep bruising also take too long, but by this point it's impatience rather than fear: incredibly, we're all fine. My daughter comes healthily four months later.

The encounter and pregnancy instill me with an unforgettable awareness of the delicacy of our bodies compared to our machines. It haunts my thoughts—hot engine smells and cars too close in front of me on the highway flood me with panicky adrenaline and flashbacks for years after. I think about the two young men from my high school class who have been killed in vehicle accidents—a four percent mortality rate for my cohort of fifty-three in under ten years. I dwell on roadkill. I remember the dog I saw get hit and killed, imagine the moment of heat and force, try to forget the sight of the owner picking up the body as blood dripped from the mouth. I often feel gratitude for my childhood cat, who had her hips broken by a car collision but survived and lived for another eighteen years.

I think about machines obliterating biology, burning away relationships and connections in an instant.

I remember the gray whale whose end came from a great engine on an unwavering path.

On Grayland Beach, the responders finish their collecting. At the table, I've been writing down the names of various organs and their destinations. The stranding responders have been handing me sliced bits of tissue, heavy as meat cutlets, to seal in plastic. Before the tide comes in, however, they have one more task, and I can't avoid it to record data this time.

The Westport Aquarium, located just north of Grayland, is interested in acquiring the whale's bones for display. They plan to bury the bones over the winter so that decay can clean them of flesh, but first, we need to free them.

I sink my body, small and alive, into the task of deconstructing this other. I stab a giant knife into her skin and saw down, in and out, to cut through thick blubber. I slam the point of the meat hook into the top of the rectangle of flesh and jerk-jerk-jerk my body, convulsing all my musculature, straining.

Slowly, very slowly, the layers of skin are pulled open like drawbridges. We see all of her ribcage, then her spine down her tail. The soft apparatus of living is stripped away. I behold her giant bones, giant skeleton, can't help but feel reverence for her even in death. No match for the machine of industrial civilization.

I find her years later on Westport Aquarium's Facebook page. I don't live in Washington anymore, so I can't visit in person; my relationship has been reduced to pixels and scrolling and clicks to see captions.

Scrolling-scrolling-scrolling through years of photos, I see them interring then extracting her bones from thick, damp, coastal forest soil, where microbes and invertebrates do the job of cleaning her skeleton. Then I see her, laid out, giant still, on tables in the little aquarium's interior.

Posters and tanks surround her, trying to educate visitors about her former world in the living seas.

I hope her death means something. I hope people reach for her bones like I reached for her dead flesh, yearning for connection even though she can't participate anymore.

Later in the year, I read about an epidemic of dead gray whales washed up on the Pacific coast, looking emaciated and malnourished. Not ships this time, but starvation. One adult male, which normally would feed on bottom-dwelling invertebrates, had a belly full of sea grass like a person trying to stave off hunger by eating lawn grass.[4] Cascadia reports thirty dead whales in Washington (the average is about six strandings per year).[5] The National Oceanic and Atmospheric Administration declares an "Unusual Mortality Event" for 2019.[6]

During my scientific training on the Pacific Northwest coast, I get to visit the ocean a lot. Every time I do, I search the waters obsessively for cetaceans, desperate to see one in the wild. Born in the middle of the continent, I never got the chance until I moved to Washington for school. But I longed for it. Vaporous breath, vital and sudden. Sleek, silvered skin. Undulation of powerful musculature, graceful as dancers. Awareness and connection in curious gazes from laterally-arranged eyes. Dolphins, whales, porpoises: I loved them without even being with them.

On my first trip whale-watching, I am glued to the railing, eyes scanning, heart racing.

In Puget Sound, on a sunlit day of glittering blue water and distant fir forests and snowcapped mountains, I see a small group of gray whales for the first time. Their breath, sulfurous and pale, catches the light. A thick wet gasp as they take that one essential gulp of air. Their backs shine. They seem to slow, wait, allow our little whale-watching boat to catch up.

A whale spy-hops out of the water. Its thick body bobs up, head clear of the waves, eye turned toward us. It sinks back down with an oddly delicate splash. I hang over the edge, mouth sore from smiling.

The whale spy-hops a few more times, then leaves. The gray whales feed from the bottom of the Sound, dredging up benthic shellfish. They come to the surface to rest and breathe for a while then dive back down for several minutes to collect prey. We press on as the waves clear of giants.

---

1. "Blue Whale Ship Strikes." Cascadia Research Collective, "Projects."

2. Yong, Ed. "North Atlantic Right Whales Are Dying in Horrific Ways." The Atlantic, June 27, 2019.

3. Beswick, Aaron. "'We can save them': NOAA researcher optimistic about N. Atlantic right whales." The Chronicle Herald, November 11, 2018.

4. "Thousands of whales are dying. Scientists have run out of public beaches for the carcasses to rot." USA Today, June 21, 2019.

5. "Cascadia Continues to Investigate Record Number of Strandings." Cascadia Research Collective, June 26, 2019.

6. "2019 Gray Whale Unusual Mortality Event Along the West Coast." NOAA Fisheries Website.

Starlings on the Interstate Bridge.
Oregon Department of Transportation, 2009.

Reading the Book of Isaiah While Wild Fires Continue to Burn
Jory Mickelson

It is summer and my church
is made of birds

winged god
in lenticular view, as if to define

ape could set
a form, a boundary to

the fathomless, a name

made of syllables *lifted*
to *blue rudiment.*

The seraphs were proto-
types for six-legged flyers:

sweat bee, salmon fly, hooktip moth,
caught in the hem, a hymn

of his robe, wind greening through leaves.

Then a raiment: "to array,"
to be adorned with rain.

We adore water amid drought,
how dryness precipitates

a leaner devotion:
the narrow path amid dust

or needle duff and still

from May to August the bark
beetle works its faith

cloistered to the inner gallery
of fir, until it too

has earned its glorious
crown. We want

the holy heat without

the flame. Isaiah warned
that at the sound

of the angels' voices, the thresholds
shook, the temple filled

with smoke—that no winged thing
can save. That the lengthening

of days may also be the end.

italicized line from "Susurrus Stanzas" by Brian Teare in Companion Grasses

Glory Glory Hallelujah
Katherine D. Morgan

God told me that He knew that I loved you before I ever said it out loud. It wasn't His fault for reading my thoughts, since He's all knowing and whatnot. He knew that I'd been holding back, watching as I chewed on the syllables, grinding them in between my teeth long before the words came out. I used to choke on them every time I saw you, swallowing hard as the phrase attempted to escape. When it finally did, you asked "What took you so long?" and I said that I'd been hoping that you'd say it first. Truth be told, what I really needed was a sign. I needed to know that you were still going to see someone worthy of your love even when I didn't. I needed to know that you could still love me at my worst, because sometimes, my worst is all that I am. But instead of saying all that shit, I texted you every couple of weeks and asked if you still liked me. Even though I always expected a "No," you'd enthusiastically respond "I do," which personally, I like to believe is foreshadowing, but God tells me not to get ahead of myself and to delete the Pinterest board or to at least make it private. Even after all this, I still don't know if I believe in God, but maybe I can learn to believe in Anything or Anyone who has brought me someone as good as you. What's so hard about believing in something you can't see or touch, but that you can feel? God nods, agreeing. Hallelujah indeed.

*Girl on tricycle at Hazel substation, 1959.
City Light Negatives (Record Series 1204-01), Seattle Municipal Archives.*

Dash

Aaron Fullerton

I tap each knee two times. I don't mean to do it, but it's become habit. I wish I could remember to stop myself because that would really piss off Dallas, but it's too ingrained in me at this point. I double knot my shoelaces. I stretch my upper body (arms, shoulders, neck, torso) then my lower body (hips, quads, Achilles, calves). I touch the start line with my toes—that's when I tap each knee two times and place my feet in the starting block. I've done it so many times now that it feels impossible to interrupt it or change it in any way. It would be like trying to spell my own name incorrectly.

My name. I used to want to change that, too, but I've given up. I was only six when Dallas convinced my mother to rename me Dash and I resented it for years, refusing to answer to it. But now it actually feels right and I can't even remember who Genny was. When I see the name on old documents sometimes, I don't connect the word, the literal sequence of those five letters, to myself. It feels like it describes nondescript seed, something that's completely meaningless beyond its potential to become something else. Once the world started seeing me as Dash, it became natural to see myself that way. When crowds are chanting "Dash!" or when it's painted across banners in big thick letters, you want to be that word that makes them so excited. I brought up Genny less and less, and then, once I heard Josie Franc say my name on her program, I knew I wanted to be Dash forever.

Josie Franc has large almond eyes and does her long auburn hair in a French braid that swings back and forth as she walks, brushing the back of her navy windbreaker. She used to be a collegiate sports correspondent for the top media conglomerate in the country and she quickly became one of their most popular reporters. Even people who never really cared about sports like track and field fell in love with her. Her interviews were her most-watched segments. She was warm with her subjects, but never at the cost of letting them off the hook. She'd create a friendly environment to get their guard down, then she'd ask the really difficult questions and she wouldn't let anyone weasel their way out of the truth. After negotiations with her employer broke down, Josie went independent and started her own online network, *Franc Conversation*, now one of the most viewed networks in sports media—getting interviewed by Josie is a huge milestone for any athlete.

Stupidly, I think: maybe today's the day she interviews me.

As I settle into position, the pads of my fingers graze the textured polyurethane of the track. I press my feet into the starting block, my legs becoming coiled springs, and I feel like if I aim myself just right I could shoot myself to the moon. I find something about 30 meters ahead of me to stare at. There's a little bit of gray discoloration on the track that will work. I focus my eyes on it and then I wait, knowing that I will push myself to that little spot of gray with the force of a jet engine. I will build on my power through the next 120 meters, my limbs moving with extreme precision, like steam-fueled pistons. In the last 50 meters, I will do a complete inventory of all the energy left inside my body, and use every last microgram of it to propel me down the straightaway, the balls of my feet sending me on a perfect horizontal trajectory, and by the time I reach the finish line and there are no competitors in my peripheral vision, I will feel like I'm flying.

And then the gun goes off and that's exactly what happens.

I set the world record.

I grab some water and catch my breath and give nods of respect to the other runners. A few of them won't look at me. One of the race managers hands out bananas and another gives us all our phones back. I eat the banana and log into my phone, but I can't stop looking over to the media pit, to where Josie Franc is standing with her cameraman. It's sunny today and she's wearing a white visor and she looks like a sailing coach. I hope that she'll call me over.

But instead, she motions for Dallas. He knew this was coming. He and my mother were already eagerly pressing against the rope to the media pit and the moment that Josie waves him over, he ducks under it and heads straight to her, pushing other reporters' microphones out of the way. He's going to give Josie the exclusive, of course. He probably negotiated it with her a week ago.

I pull up Josie's channel on my phone and watch the interview live. As Josie lightly turns her microphone toward Dallas—a graceful bit of practiced choreography—I catch myself in the deep background of the shot. There I am, behind Josie and Dallas, watching Josie and Dallas. People sometimes tell me my life must be surreal, and I say, "No, not really," but in moments like this, when I feel like I'm completely inside my own head but also wholly outside my own body, I guess I know what they mean.

Dallas shoots Josie a proud smile. He talks to her like she's an old friend—which makes sense, because this is the fourth time she's interviewed him. "You know, I can't say I never imagined this," Dallas says and Josie's eyebrows raise as she nods. "This was always one of the goals for Dash. World record in the 200. She's been training non-stop."

"But of course," Josie chimes in, "it's a little disingenuous to chalk it all up to the training."

Dallas looks down and smiles. It's a move he learned from his favorite actor, who always acts very humble when giving acceptance speeches. Dallas had to learn how to be humble by watching someone else, because he's never felt humble for a single second of his entire life.

"Well, yes, the coding can't be discounted," Dallas says, acting like it only just occurred to himself to give his sequence some credit. "That is true."

"Other geneticists have been trying to replicate your coding for almost a generation now, but Dash is still the gold standard for genetic editing, at least for speed. Now that she's broken her second world record, are you more inclined to share the secrets of your sequence, or do you feel that much more pressure to keep it under lock and key?"

Dallas performs a light little laugh, but I don't know what I'm supposed to think he finds funny about the question. After a moment of pretending to really internalize her question, he says, "Dash is special. She's not just the sum of my edits. There's so much hard work involved every day. From both of us."

I knew he was going to say "from both of us," but it still makes my blood boil when I actually hear it. Josie starts to take the microphone back, but then he adds a little more: "When I finished perfecting the sequence, I knew that that was the beginning of my journey with Dash, not the end. That's what the other amateur geneticists out there need to understand."

I'm so enraged I throw my banana peel on the track and I smash it into the track with the heel of my shoe. I immediately worry that Josie's audience saw me in the background of the shot but when I check the interview again, I see that the cameraman has shifted the angle and I'm now completely hidden by Dallas' giant head.

Dallas has a big grin on his face. I can see it in the rearview mirror from the backseat. He catches me looking and narrows his eyes. "Don't pout." I'm immediately embarrassed. I wonder if my face is that transparent, or if Dallas intuited my state of mind. More often than not, Dallas is able to simply look at me and know exactly how I'm feeling, even if I haven't been able to fully articulate it to myself yet. It's like he's hacked my brain and taken over my inner monologue and I'm just constantly playing catch up, autofilling the ends of his statements about me.

I know that there's nothing too special about Dallas' ability to know what I'm thinking and feeling. He's just observant. He's been paying close attention to me since I was born. Well, actually, since before I was born. More than my mother and sometimes even more than myself, he's aware of who I am and what I need. It drives me insane because he's almost always right. So I often tell him he's wrong, because I think it'll make him ashamed, but he always knows that I'm lying, and then it's me who feels ashamed.

And that's exactly what happens. "I'm not p-p-pouting," I say as I turn my eyes toward the window. Dallas turns to my mother and they share a knowing a look, although my mother doesn't put much effort into it because she's too busy screengrabbing stills from Dallas' interview with Josie. She'll print them out later for her scrapbook.

The shame of being caught in a lie starts to come over me like a shadow, so I try to explain it all away. "I'm just disap-p-p-poin-pointed that I didn't get to talk about my r-r-race."

Dallas presses his tongue into the back of his teeth, a sure sign that he's annoyed to have to explain something he thought was already clear. He may have learned all of my habits and giveaways, but I've learned plenty of his, too. "So, let's imagine this again, shall we? Josie holds up the microphone to your mouth and asks you how it feels to set the world record. What do you say?"

I freeze up. Normally, Dallas just explains the situation away so we can move on to another topic. Switching it around on me is a new tactic. I squirm in my seat, unprepared for this line of attack. His eyes meet mine in the mirror again: "Well?"

"I… I tell her that I feel—"

"No, don't explain it to me. Pretend she's here in the car and she just asked you the question. And you say…"

I turn to my mother for back-up, but she's oblivious to the discussion. And I know that every second of my silence is a victory for Dallas, so I launch into the answer. "J-J-Josie, thank you s-s-so much for asking about that. I'm deeply p-p-p-proud, but there's still… I have work to d-d-do…" And then I shut up. Because I've proven his point and we both know it. If my stammer is this out of control right here in the car, we can only imagine how bad it would be if I was actually standing next to Josie, looking at her big eyes and the zig zag of the French braid across the top of her head. I'd probably be completely unintelligible.

"You and Dallas make such a good team!" my mother suddenly says without looking up. "You handle the actual physical feat and he articulates your success beautifully." Perhaps she was listening all along. "I know no one calls short-distance running a team sport, but maybe you should think of it like a team sport, and Dallas is your teammate. Like a relay!"

Dallas beams at my mother, places his hand on her thigh. "I think that's a beautiful sentiment, my dear." Then he looks at me in the rearview again. "We'll get a mountain of written interview requests tomorrow, anyway. You'll be able to use all of those to discuss the race."

My mother suddenly looks up. She shoves her phone toward Dallas, showing him a screengrab. She explains to him that it's the best one and I shift between the seats to get a look at it and I have to agree. Josie's in profile and she has a big smile on her face, like she couldn't be more excited to have witnessed my historic run.

That night, after the nutritionist and the sports masseuse leave, my mother asks if she can do something with my hair. I nod. I don't know what she's planning on doing with it, but I trust her well enough.

I sit on the ground, ice packs on my legs. She sits above me on the couch and turns on some Curtis Mayfield, but keeps the volume really low, so it sounds like it's a few rooms away. She always does this. I think she likes the way it makes it feel like there's a party happening nearby, and we don't need to have been invited, it's just enough to know there's a party and people are having a good time. When "So in Love" comes on, we both sing along to it. I can usually sing through the first couple verses without a single stammer.

She gets to work on my hair, tugging, and I feel an immediate sharp pain in my scalp, but it's a pain that's so familiar and connected to my mother's process that I don't even classify it as pain. It feels more like love.

She doesn't say anything and I don't either, but I'm thinking about asking her about my father, which I always think about in the rare quiet moments we have together. I know she's probably wondering if that's what I'm thinking about. I can sense, in the silence, her steeling herself just in case.

It's been a few years now since I last asked about him. I had gotten into an argument with Dallas about the color of my shoes and, I hate to admit it, but I don't even remember what color I was arguing for or against. We were at the gym when things got heated, and I shouted "Fuck you, Dallas!" right in his face, but I stammered on the F and over the course of just three words—just four fucking syllables!—my act of defiance transformed into a moment of humiliation. I stormed off and raced home to my room, where I started searching online for how to cure stammering. I knew that my elongated quadriceps had come from Dallas' genetic meddling, but where the hell did my stammer come from?

I had zero solid leads when my mother entered the room. Thinking that maybe there was a simple explanation for the origin of my impediment, I looked her in the eye and told her to tell me about my real father. I was operating on a full tank of spite so I probably didn't ask very kindly.

I knew very little about him at that point. All I knew, actually, was that he was dead. And I only knew this because I had heard Dallas tell the story so many times to so many reporters. The story always went like this:

I was visiting a friend of mine, an OBGYN and fertility specialist, because I felt that I had perfected my sequences but I wanted another set of eyes on it, specifically a set of eyes who'd better understand the practical process of implementing them. And while I was waiting for him to get a break between patients, this luminous woman stepped into the lobby.

(If my mother was with him during the interview, he'd turn to her and smile at this point and she would squeeze his hand and blush.)

She was luminous, yes, but there was also a profound sadness to her. I couldn't help myself—I had to know why this beautiful creature seemed so heartbroken. I took the chair next to her and asked if she was alright and she told me that shortly after getting pregnant, the child's father had died. And now she was four months along and she was so scared to raise this baby by herself. She was struggling to find hope and stability and—I'll never forget this—she said she needed a sense of purpose. Not just for herself but for her child. It was like she was an angel that had been sent into my life, but I think, after I explained what I was planning to do, maybe she thought that I was the angel who was sent to her. Because purpose is what I was offering, although I'm not sure I thought of it that way at the time.

So, when I finally confronted my mom, that's all I really knew. He died right after he donated his genetic material to the cause of me being born. That wasn't enough for me anymore. I wanted her to give me something precious and incredible. I wanted a hero story. What I wanted most was to hear that he was special in a way that Dallas was not. I wanted a man, even if it was just an idea of a man, to whom Dallas could never measure up. And then I wanted to find ways to wound Dallas with that information.

I waited for my mother to say something. It took her quite a while to formulate her answer. I watched her thinking, rearranging words and ideas in her head as she stood in place in my doorway, staring into the trophy case in the corner of the room, the sun hitting a few of them so that they flung golden geometry across her face.

She took a deep breath: "He died in the war, Dash. Do you know how hard that was?" Her voice was hollow and metallic. "I need this to be the end of the conversation." I nodded my head and she left me alone, closing the door behind her.

I curled up onto my bed, sealing myself in a cocoon of shame. I had never recognized that my mother's life was missing such an essential piece. I had never known my father and I had never tried to understand who my mother might have been when he was around. I had never considered that parts of her may have died right along with him and that grief had worked her over like sandpaper, smoothing her out and simplifying the shapes of her personality. The combination of my mom and Dallas and me had always felt like a complete unit, but I could suddenly see that wasn't quite true. There was this giant empty space in my mother's life, and I had always looked right through it, focusing my angry gaze on Dallas.

Confused by the revelation and simmering in a stew of guilt and self-pity, I wasn't sure if I wanted to nurture or be nurtured. I searched the house for my mother and found her on the pale blue sofa by the window and I sat at her feet. I had never done that before, but it felt right. Later, I wondered if I was acting submissive as an unspoken plea for forgiveness or if I just wanted to make myself seem small and childlike to play on her maternal instincts.

She rubbed her hand gently over the top of my head. "It's time to do something new with your hair," she said. I sat at her feet for hours as she had her way with it.

As I fell asleep later that night, I realized I didn't know if my father was a soldier or a civilian or who-knows-what. And I had no idea what war she was talking about.

Every time she does my hair now, I know she's waiting for me to ask those follow-up questions but I've never been able to get the words out. And then "So in Love" will come on and we'll sing together and when it's over, we'll both feel relieved.

Dallas was right. A mountain of written interview requests comes in. Or so he says. Everything flows through him, so I don't know how many actually come in, but I know that there are at least six requests from prestigious publications because he forwards me their questions with a message that says, "These are the only ones worth responding to."

I flip through them and they're all variations on the same questions over and over. *When I was running, was I thinking about the record? When did I realize I had beaten it? What special rituals or superstitions play into my running routine? What's next for Dash?* I've often wondered if journalists always ask the most boring and basic questions or if Dallas only forwards me the blandest questions possible. I asked him about this once and he patted me on the back and chuckled.

I start typing my answers and I copy and paste them into similar questions across the six interviews. Then I go through and rearrange sentences in different answers. I look up words in the thesaurus and change ones here and there so that no two journalists are getting the exact same response. Every time I do this, I wonder if this is what it was like for Dallas when he edited my genetic sequences. Did it feel like moving around punctuation and playing with word choice until he ended up with me, his Perfect Sentence?

I'm working on an answer about how I keep my focus, but as I type it up I realize that I said almost the exact thing last time I broke a world record. I go online and do a quick search of some of my past interviews to make sure I'm not repeating myself too egregiously. As I scroll through, it suddenly occurs to me that I've never actually read them before. Dallas has always encouraged me not to pay attention to news about myself and even though I push back against everything he says, this seemed like particularly sound advice for me. I think I had always assumed, though, that when I sent my answers back to the journalists, they just posted everything as I had written it. I expected it to look like a generic Q&A. In my head, I assumed that they were copying and pasting my answers from the email into the article in the same way that I was copying and pasting my answers from one reply to the next.

But none of them were like that. They were all long, in-depth articles about my running career, and how my success marked a tipping point in how society viewed genetically edited individuals. The writers marveled at my accomplishments. More than once, my physique was described as godlike. There were breathless descriptions of how my legs move and how my ponytail becomes nearly horizontal by my third step. There were allusions to the fact that I rarely ever speak in public and a few theories about why that is, ranging from shyness to monk-like humility to an ambiguous philosophy about "letting the speed speak for itself."

And I shouldn't have been surprised, but there was so much about Dallas. Dallas' pithy quotes were splashed across the articles or paraphrased in their titles. There were photos of him in a track jacket looking off into the distance, his furrowed brow suggesting he was deep in thought. There were photos of him in an expensive suit and track shoes, posing inside a giant double helix statue made from scrap metal. Sometimes, these photos were posted right next to mine, as if to say, "Here is the Brain, and here is the Brawn." Most of the articles treated Dallas with great reverence; one writer went so far as to call him the "spiritual heir to Jonas Salk and Thomas Edison." A couple articles seemed to imply a whiff of suspicion, however, and delicately addressed the initial reluctance of collegiate sports to let me participate and, more interestingly to me, the mixed public reaction to Dallas' successful edits.

I was only peripherally aware of the fact that, when I was little, my very existence was a bit controversial. The rise of in-utero genetic editing was seen as a way to prevent birth defects or susceptibility to certain diseases, but once the tech went commercial, amateurs could play around with it. No one really expected anyone to start building super-humans, but anything was theoretically on the table. "It was the Wild West," as one article put it. Dallas had been a competitive runner in college but often finished in the back half of all his races. He believed that, with the right embryo, he could edit together the perfect runner. Well, I was that embryo and Dallas' edits became the most famous secret recipe since Coca-Cola.

After reading the articles, I looked up the names of some of the organizations or political figures who had condemned Dallas. They had said pretty vicious stuff fifteen years ago, stuff that made even me bristle. It was unusual, the experience of feeling sympathy toward Dallas. A few people compared him to Nazi doctors, suggesting that he violated the Nuremberg Code. "Mad scientist trying to play God" was a common refrain, as was "Dr. Frankenstein."

A few critics bypassed the ethical and went straight to the personal, calling Dallas' feat a transparent and cynical quest for the glory that had eluded him in his youth. These charges seemed so ugly, mostly because they echoed my own darkest analyses of Dallas. To see some of my harshest judgements of Dallas in print—written by someone I had never met—gave me the odd sensation of having been violated. If anyone should get to crystallize negative opinions of Dallas on the time capsule of the internet, it should be me—but others had beaten me to it. They had stolen my sentiments and made them more cutting. They took my fleeting, angry thoughts and gave them the gravity of truth. Maybe they were truth.

But when I look at what these critics said now, nearly everyone has changed their tunes. They all begrudgingly accept the churn of human progress and the value of "looking past traditional self-imposed so-called ethical barriers." Dallas has won them over with his charm and his constant emphasis on the idea that genetics only get you so far. "Ninety-nine percent of success comes down to hard work and smart training" was a Dallas quote that popped up in a few different articles.

I read article after article after article. Some from now, some from years ago, some from apologists, some from supporters, some from staunch resistors. And after that initial discomfort of seeing writers echo some of my most hateful secret thoughts, what took over was a profound, hollow sadness. Not a single person—no journalist or academic or activist—had made any attempt to capture my personality. They all mentioned me as if I was a concept, a walking (or running) challenge to the old ways of thinking about human ability. I represented ideas that were beautiful or terrifying or complicated, but who was I? No one seemed to care. Maybe that's because Dallas limited their access to me, sure, but they also didn't even ruminate about my life outside of running. They certainly made no attempts to understand it. A speeding bullet, after all, has no dreams or hopes or vulnerabilities—it only has its destiny. I would have given over my whole heart to read a sentence that marveled at my smile instead of my calf muscles.

I was desperate to find something like that, some kind of validation that I wasn't Dallas' pet or project or robot because hell, I wasn't even his daughter. I was just a very fast young woman who liked strawberry milkshakes and Korean animation and Curtis Mayfield and yellow headbands and Josie Franc.

Josie Franc.

I knew that a lot of my fans were big Josie-watchers, so I figured if I looked through the comments on some of her videos about me, I'd find some compliments, which I really needed. Of course, with a comments section, there's always the risk of stumbling upon the most disgusting thoughts people could form, but I was feeling brave. I hoped that if I found vitriol, it'd at least be aimed at Dallas. Every interview, after all, was with him, not me.

I scrolled through pages of comments and most of them were just about Josie and how great she looked in the visor. I couldn't disagree with those and, since I was logged in under an anonymous account, I even hit the thumbs-up button on a few of them. There were some about my training regimen and some about the excitement of witnessing history and a lot of comments about how the world record probably won't last very long since the government will build someone even faster any day now.

But there was one comment that seemed to float away from the others and it had generated its own discussion thread.

"i have a theory," it said. "dallas seems like one of those guys who acts all humble but really loves glory. so what i think is when he was editing dash, he started to think he'd have to share the glory with her. he hated that. he wanted all the credit. so he edited her to be mute too, so that she can't talk about her running and he gets to do all the interviews and be all visible and get the glory."

My head was already swirling as I read the discussion points below. A few people posted footage of me and Dallas chatting on the practice track and, even though it was too far away to hear anything, it was clear that I wasn't mute. Someone even mentioned a "rumor" that I had shouted "Fuck you!" at Dallas at a practice years ago.

The original poster responded: "ok, fine, she can talk but maybe he did something to her genes to make her not wanna talk."

A sound came out of me, from deep in my gut. It felt like a scream, but it sounded like a sigh.

The next few days, leading up to the 400m, I couldn't think about anything else. But Dallas made the rare mistake of misreading me. He appreciated that I seemed singularly focused. In all our training exercises, I never pushed back against him or complained. I executed all the drills with a precision that can only be attributed to muscle memory. The idea that Dallas had edited my stammer into me had soaked through to my bone marrow and it had turned me into the machine that Dallas had always wished I was.

We were at the practice track for hours every day, so I could only check on the comment thread late at night and first thing in the morning. I would refresh and refresh, hoping other users would elaborate on the theory or maybe someone would emerge with incontrovertible proof. But no one did. Someone replied "doubt it" and another accused the original user of peddling conspiracies. The only time I got a jolt of satisfaction was when I saw the post get more Likes, and even that was a rare occurrence.

I wasn't sure what to do. I couldn't confront Dallas about it—I'd never get the truth. I could make a public accusation, but Dallas could shut that down too since I had nothing but angry ideas and gut feelings. I could go looking for evidence, but who knows how long that would take?

Or if it even exists? I couldn't go on simmering like this for much longer.

I had to cleave myself from Dallas. I had become—no, I was *designed* to be—the blue ox, a magical creature who's only present to prop up a man's mythological reputation. Well, the ox deserves a few stories of its own, I think. It's a magical fucking ox. But how does it get the world to ignore Paul Bunyan for a few minutes?

The idea came to me in a dream. I was carrying a baby in my arms and I was running through the house, looking for my mother because I knew, somehow, that it was hers. I could hear her voice in another room, but every time I entered it, she wasn't there.

I was starting to panic and it felt like the baby was going to slip out of my hands. It was wrapped up tight in a smooth, shiny fabric and I couldn't get a good grip on it. I kept holding it tighter to my chest which felt so wrong and uncomfortable because my arms shouldn't be stationary while I run.

I followed the sound of her voice into the kitchen, but she wasn't there either. In her place was Dallas, standing at the refrigerator, wearing an apron. He reached out and I knew he wanted the baby. I was so scared of handing the baby over to him but I was more scared that I would drop it and my dream instincts kicked in and I gave the baby to Dallas. He smiled at me sweetly and patted my head, just like my mother would, and then he slid the baby into the oven.

I woke up at 2AM, sweat on my forehead. I wiped it off with the corner of my sheet and tiptoed out into the hallway, the sense of panic still alive in my bloodstream. I went downstairs and found my supply bag for the race, doing my best to be as quiet as possible. Dallas and I had packed it already, putting all my essentials in it, so that in the morning we could just grab the bag and head straight to the race.

I pulled out my participation bib, the piece of paper that runners pin to our chests and, with the embedded microchip, pinpoints our exact times. Unlike my competitors, my bib displays my first name—which, really, has become my only name. Dallas negotiated this with the athletic association several years ago and now, staring at these four letters, it looks like a joke all over again. She's a sprinter and her name is Dash. A flash of righteous anger rises inside me as I think of all those articles that praise his creativity when here I am, staring at the most obvious evidence of his laziness.

I flip the bib over and, with a magic marker, I write across it in big block letters: "MY NAME IS GENNY."

I slide it into the bag, exactly where it was before, and then I go back to bed and I fall asleep immediately.

In the morning, I come downstairs to get breakfast before we leave and Dallas and my mother are waiting for me at the kitchen island. My mother has a half-eaten bowl of cereal in front of her as she stares into the marble countertop like she's trying to decode the swirls and shapes in it. Dallas, though, is standing and looking right at me and for a split-second, I get a little confused and think maybe I'm still in the dream. He has an aggressive energy about him and I feel like he could shove a baby in the oven if I handed him one.

I reach into the fridge for an electrolyte water and ask them if everything's OK. Dallas sighs and when I close the fridge door, I see him reaching behind the island for something. He pulls up the bib.

So it wasn't a great plan, I guess.

The confrontation of it, of having my secret plan presented to me as not-so-secret, sends a wave of adrenaline through me that makes me very confident and very nervous at the same time. I ask Dallas why he was looking through the bag, quickly casting myself as the wronged party.

"I triple check our supplies every morning before a race," he says. Which is probably true. So now I feel like an idiot.

He holds up the bib, my big block letters stained across it. "Can you explain to us what this is all about?"

I think about lying, but I can see Dallas watching me thinking about lying and it makes the whole thing feel stupid. So I just talk.

I tell him that I think he gave me the stammer on purpose so that I wouldn't talk to reporters, so that he can take credit for all my wins, and if I'm not Dash any more than maybe everything will change. When I'm done saying it all, I feel like I just pushed a truck off a cliff.

I wait for Dallas to speak but it's my mother who jumps in first. "He didn't do that."

I ask how she's so sure.

But it's Dallas who answers this time. "I wouldn't even know where to begin. I wanted you to be fast and, honestly, I didn't really care about anything else." It almost sounds like an apology, but I've never heard him apologize so I can't be sure. He taps his fingers across the marble. Bum-bum-bum-bum. Bum-bum-bum-bum. "Speed was my only focus so I only made genetic alterations that would benefit your speed. It's as simple as that."

I try to ask how he expects me to just take his word for it, but I struggle to get the words out and halfway through, he interrupts me. "Stammers and stutters and speech impediments aren't even necessarily genetic."

He's being so calm. I hate how calm he is. If anyone was watching, they'd think I'm the unreasonable one.

"Sure, sometimes it can be genetic, but it can also be caused by early childhood trauma or all kinds of other environmental factors. You're ascribing bad intentions to something that's just bad luck."

I feel tears rolling down my face. I don't know when I started crying. I shout that I wasn't traumatized and then I quickly amend that, saying that if I was traumatized, it was probably by Dallas.

"OK," Dallas says, rolling his eyes with his voice. "Whatever you want to believe. Unless you want to believe that I gave it to you on purpose."

I turn my face away. I don't like him seeing me cry but, even more importantly, I don't want him to read my expression. Because I believe him. I hate myself for believing him, but I do and I don't want him to know that. I want him to writhe eternally in the discomfort of not knowing.

And it works. I hear the anger rising in his voice. "I'm not some sociopathic evil mastermind. What I don't think you realize is that I rescued you. I gave you a life and I've been a father to you."

I turn suddenly and shout at him. "My f-f-f-father was a war hero!"

Dallas' head flickers on his neck, a flame on a wick. "What are you talking about?"

Then my mother vomits her cereal across the countertop.

We all stand in place for a long moment, as if my mother has simply redesigned the kitchen and we're all taking it in before offering our opinions. Dallas grabs a roll of paper towels, tears a few off and tosses the rest of the roll to my mother. She fumbles the catch, drops them to the floor. He runs the towels under the faucet, wetting them and as he wipes down the counter, his eyes drill into the top of my mother's head because she refuses to look up. "Did you tell her that? That he's a war hero?"

I jump in before my mother can say anything. I explain that my mother simply said he died in the war and nothing more than that. The whole "hero" part was an assumption on my end.

Dallas throws up his hands, one of which still contains a vomit-soaked paper towel. "What is going on around here?"

I can't quite explain it, but my mother's vomit seems to have reset the energy in the room. Somehow, I'm sturdier and Dallas is more off-balance and I feel like I need to take advantage. I do my best to match his annoyingly calm tone from earlier and tell Dallas that it's only natural that I would seek answers to my past and if he's surprised by the situation, then maybe he was never prepared to raise a child that wasn't his in the first place. I think of all that in the moment and I add a little bite to it at the end and I'm very proud of myself. I've never felt more like an adult.

And I guess it came off as well as I thought because Dallas looks utterly defeated. He takes a seat at the counter beside my mother and he deflates. My mother still won't look up at him.

"You're right."

I kind of can't believe it.

"We always agreed that we'd tell you the truth but we just kept putting it off. You became so… well, you exceeded all expectations. And I didn't want you exposed to information that could knock you off your path. I'm not sure that earns me any forgiveness, but I hope it at least helps you understand."

This is why Dallas is so good in interviews. Even when he's apologizing, even when he's admitting to a major fuck-up, he still finds a way to make it seem classy. I hate it so much.

"W-w-what war d-d-did he die in?" I blurt out.

Dallas shoots another look to my mother even though we both know she won't look up. It's just for my sake, to remind me that I should be blaming her just as much as I'm blaming him.

"There was no war. Well, there were plenty of wars, I suppose, but your father didn't die in any of them. Your father was one of my teammates from college. He and your mother had a, um, well, a brief relationship…"

There go his fingers. Bum-bum-bum-bum. Bum-bum-bum-bum.

"And anyway, well, he was killed in a robbery a couple weeks after your mother ended things."

My knees start to buckle. I lean against the fridge for balance. I ask how the robbers killed him. If they were caught.

"Well, no, see. Your dad actually was the robber. He broke into an electronics store in the middle of the night and he shot at the security guard and the security guard shot back at him and hit him in the neck."

My mother vomits a little bit more.

"But he and I had been teammates in college and he was a great runner. Raw talent and great technique. I went to his funeral and that's where

Fullerton • 69

I met your mother." His head flickers again. "Well, actually, no, that's not true. I just heard about your mother at the funeral. I heard someone mention that your father might live on because his ex was having a baby, but then someone else said your mother was planning to terminate the pregnancy."

I scratch at my scalp. Not hard enough to produce blood, but maybe if I keep at it for a while.

"The circumstances, for me, were pretty ideal. An embryo that already had great genetic material to begin with and would make the editing a little simpler. I just had to convince your mother to keep you. And lucky for you, Dash, I'm very convincing."

Dallas grabs the roll of paper towels off the floor—the ones my mother had dropped—and starts wiping up the vomit again. He seems relaxed, like the conversation is over. Like he's the one who got to push the truck off a cliff.

I stop scratching at my scalp and check my fingers for blood, but there's nothing. I slide to the floor, my back still against the fridge, and I slowly drink my electrolyte water, one sip at a time. After a couple minutes, my mother grabs her cereal bowl and puts it in the sink and slides away into another room like she's an air hockey puck. But Dallas just keeps cleaning the counter, spraying it with disinfectant and getting it to gleam.

I finish my water and I crush the plastic bottle in my hand because it's the only way I can think to express my anger. But it's not the anger I want—I'm angry because I'm not angrier about everything. I can now righteously and accurately claim to be the victim, but my victimhood requires my mother's villainy and that's a riptide I can't step into, not yet. Not today.

I want to hate that I've been lied to. I wish I could say it destroyed my life, but the truth is, deep down, I want the lie back. I crave the simple mystery of the lie and I feel childish for wanting it and I feel even more childish for all the times I dreamed of better stories for myself. I wanted to feel like the lie had trapped me in some way, but it had done the opposite. It had freed my imagination and allowed me to see all the potential in myself.

But then I find a little fleck of anger, buried under all the other anger. It's when Dallas said he gave me a life. And I water that fleck and I nourish it and now I see my victimhood in the way I want to see it. Now I see the story I can tell myself. Dallas gave me a life, sure, but he didn't give me *my* life. He gave me *his* life, and I've been unable to wrestle control of it away from him for nineteen long years. And it's a version of the story I've always clung to, but now it burns so bright with truth that it's crisp at the edges.

I stand up and I lean on the clean counter and I lock eyes with Dallas and I tell him that if I win today, I want to talk to Josie. Otherwise, I'm not going to compete. I'll walk the whole four hundred meters, make a big show out of it and embarrass us both.

Dallas doesn't quite smile, but I can hear a lift in his voice when he says, "So you still want to set the world record today?"

I still tap my knees. I really thought, on the drive to the track, as I sat in the backseat and tried to understand everything new about myself, that I definitely wouldn't tap my knees. But I did and who gives a fuck?

I lock into position in the starting block and I break down the 400 meters in my head and how I'll ease into the turns and how I'll power through the straightaways. The runner to my left sneers at me and I almost laugh, as if she can do anything to me this morning that hasn't already been done.

I breathe. Focused and alert.

The gun goes off.

I'm out in front quickly, not that I'm looking to my left and right, but I can sense the emptiness in my periphery. I charge forward and I can feel, after 50 meters, that something is off. My run is wild and unstable and I'm not sure what's happening but all that matters is that I'm moving forward as fast as possible. I keep going and I try to smooth out my gait on the turn but I overcorrect and I dip out of my lane for a split second. I've never done that before and I think, "Wow, I've never done that before" and if I'm thinking that then I'm not thinking about how fast I'm going.

And now—shit!—here are two of them, in my periphery. I push harder or, at least, I try to push harder, but I'm using everything. There's nothing else to push. As I come upon the second and final turn, I do everything I can to spread my stride and get more centimeters per step, even though I know Dallas wouldn't approve of this strategy. My stride is my stride and it comes from my height and if I try to alter it, well…

Yeah. I dip into the other lane again. But this time, because a couple runners have caught up, I step right into one. She and I smash together and we tumble down onto the track, our limbs whipping against each other, the track scraping my palms as I reach out to stop myself.

I look up just in time to see someone else win. The runner I ran into is screaming at me, her voice piercing the air like a siren, but I have no idea what she's saying. I don't hear her. I just hear an ocean of static.

I look for Dallas in the crowd and it doesn't take me long to find him. I think he'll look furious, maybe there will be actual steam coming out of his ears, but his mouth is just a sad little line and his eyes look scared. He nods at me. I just stare back. And then he nods again.

And now I see what he means. Josie Franc is rushing toward me with her microphone and her cameraman. She still has her French braid but no visor today and her windbreaker is an emerald green that matches the color of her eyes. She gives her cameraman a signal—*don't record yet*—and bends down next to me.

She's talking to me. And it's not an interview. She's talking to me like I'm just another person and her voice is all wrong. There's no honey in the tea. "Dallas, he said you'd give me an exclusive and, well… are you OK?"

I nod. I'm still on my hands and knees on the track and I realize I should probably stand up.

"OK, good, well, I want to obviously ask about what just happened. Hear your thoughts as you're processing it all. I'm sure, I'm sure it's a lot."

I nod again.

"And you're sure you're OK?"

I nod one more time.

Josie turns to her cameraman and gives a signal and the little red light comes on and, according to Josie, we're live. She explains what just happened and how, in many ways, it felt like witnessing the impossible. She says that watching me run is usually like witnessing the impossible, but watching me lose is a whole different kind of flavor. She turns to me: "So, Dash, what exactly happened out there? Can you give us the play-by-play?"

She then does the delicate choreography with the microphone where she dips it from her mouth to mine. I think about what I want to say.

But I have no idea what I want to say. And I sure as hell don't know how I'm going to say it. My lips don't open. I just stand there. I see the worry start to cloud up those beautiful green eyes of Josie's and she starts to dip her microphone back to her own mouth and all I can think about is Curtis Mayfield, the first verse of "So in Love," and that's when I finally do it.

I start to sing and nobody stops me.

Workers at Boundary Dam, 1967.
City Light Negatives (Record Series 1204-01), Seattle Municipal Archives.

Oliver de la Paz in conversation with The Poet Salon
Spring 2020

Oliver de la Paz is the author of five collections of poetry and a co-chair for Kundiman, a not-for-profit organization dedicated to promoting the work of Asian American poets. A recipient of grants from the NEA and Artist Trust, de la Paz teaches at the College of the Holy Cross and in the MFA Program at Pacific Lutheran University.

In 2020, de la Paz went on *The Poet Salon* podcast to discuss poetry, community, and his latest book, *The Boy in the Labyrinth*, which draws from myth, science, and his own experiences as a parent to explore autism, language, and development. *The Poet Salon* is hosted by *Moss* poetry editor Dujie Tahat along with Gabrielle Bates and Luther Hughes. The conversation below is edited for form and clarity.

Tahat

Let's get into this conversation. As someone born in the Philippines myself, I grew up in Eastern Washington. You also came from the Philippines and grew up in Eastern Oregon, which is like the country of the Pacific Northwest—very different from Seattle and Portland. I'm curious how you arrived at poetry, and at what point you realized it was a profession.

We arrived in the country in 1972. My parents left the Philippines after Marcos had declared martial law. And part of the reason why we had to leave the country was they were political refugees. My uncle on my father's side was blacklisted by the Marcos regime. Anyone who was blacklisted was basically a target for assassination or murder.

My dad took the temperature of the room and just said, "we've got to get the hell out. We have to get out of here." How that came to pass is an interesting story. He basically stood in line. There's a camp in the Philippines called Camp Crazy, where there was a queue about a mile long.

He waited in that line almost a week to get his visas stamped. And he finally got fed up and just threw it at the guy who was stamping visas, left, went home, got lunch, came back and found his visa stamped. We left basically that afternoon. He got a ticket to America. We packed what little we had and we flew into San Francisco, and that was it.

My mother at the time was a physician so she basically dropped her practice. She dropped everything, and she had to start over. What ended up happening is she did her residency in Virginia after San Francisco, then did her internship in Connecticut, and then purchased a practice from a lady who was retiring in Eastern Oregon.

Part of the deal back then was that in order to get her credentials, she had to serve an underserved population. So we ended up in Eastern Oregon, and basically, my father wept when he saw what the landscape looked like. And I have to say that, because of the landscape, because there was no community, that's where I retreated into books, where I retreated into my imagination. And I'm an only child, so I was always writing. Most of my time was spent by myself creating, inventing, reading.

Tahat

How did your parents take it when you told them you were going to be a poet?

de la Paz

Uh huh. Well, Filipino to Filipino: Not well at first. I mean, my dad still asks me, "Hey, why don't you take the LSAT? Why don't you get a business degree, or something like that," after all this time. I'm like, "Hello? I'm almost in my fifties. I mean, this is not going to happen, Dad."

My mom, who was a physician, took it well. She understood. She knew that I didn't really have the temperament. I had to sort of make peace with myself. You know, I did all the pre-med stuff. I did all the medical stuff. I was trying to be the dutiful son. I was an EMT for two years, in L.A. County. That was right around '93, '94, right around the L.A. riots, the Rodney King beating, all of that. It was a wild time.

Bates

You have a new book out that's very exciting, *The Boy in the Labyrinth*. I wanted to talk a little bit about that. The book opens with this almost preface piece, where you really lay the context of the book bare and talk in a pretty plainspoken way about being the father of these two boys who are on the autism spectrum.

I was wondering if you would talk about, if you're comfortable, how what you've learned about autism has affected how you think about poetry?

de la Paz

I think it's changed my relationship with the metaphor. My children don't think metaphorically—they think in terms of causation. If *this*, then *this*. With the metaphor, there's a transference. And for them, that transference doesn't happen.

But I think that it's changed how I approach writing, too. That opening piece is my way of saying, "OK, I need to back up away from the metaphor and metaphoric language and be direct here." It serves as an anchoring piece for the book, because it's so metaphorical that I think readers who don't have that context won't know that that's what I'm talking about.

So, in a nutshell, it's made me consider and scrutinize the way I'm using language. The way I'm speaking, the use of repetition has become really important, the use of clarity. So instead of metaphor, I'm using syntax. Instead of using these deep images, I'm using clarity of language, but maybe a little bit more repetition or insistence.

Hughes

I'm curious about your process for organizing and sectioning the book. How did ordering play a role in working through all these things?

de la Paz

I think that is something I came to late. The initial impetus for the book was those labyrinths of prose poems—there were a hundred of them, which was sort of an unwieldy thing to manage, and I didn't know how to approach or engage it. And so that's where that imperative came in: "I don't know how to organize this. I don't know what I'm doing." This feeling of disorder came in, and what ended up happening is, I gave it some time and distance. I walked away from it for a while. I started writing the book in 2008, so it's been on the burner for some time.

And while that was cooking, I was working on two other things, so I had an outlet to go to, but I kept being called back to this. And in terms of the organization or the structure, I didn't come to the ode structure that you might see in this until the eleventh hour.

And why the ode? I wanted to structure it in a way that was argumentative, if that makes sense. I think that the book is an argument. The book is a type of discussion that I'm having with myself and that includes whether or not I have permission to have this conversation about the subject. That's sort of what's underlying in the book. I'm arguing with myself as a father, primarily.

Tahat

Was there a clarifying moment for you, where you gave yourself the permission to be explicit? At what point did that first poem enter?

de la Paz

I went to a writing retreat residency where I was one of the teachers up in Canada, out in B.C., and Alicia Ostriker was one of the other teachers. My kids were there, and they were running around, having fun, and basically being part of the retreat experience. And Alicia Stricker knew that I wasn't writing about them or I didn't think I was writing about them.

And then she socked me in the elevator and was like, "Why aren't you writing about these kids?" And I basically asked myself that question after

I left, "Why? Why am I not writing these things?" That sort of issued fourth from me a charge that I'm going to start writing about my kids. I'm going to start engaging in the personal in ways that I hadn't before.

So that's where I started unpeeling the mask, if that makes sense. I was definitely using a mask to write these poems at the start. I think it just took a punch from Alicia Stricker.

Bates

A literal punch.

de la Paz

Sometimes a literal punch.

Bates

There's a line in *The Boy in the Labyrinth*—"The boy does not know home. Only its omission"—that makes me wonder what you think of when you think of home. And if it's something that you also think of in terms of negation.

de la Paz

It's about comfort for me. I'm a person of ritual. I like my routine. My boys are very much beings who require ritual. Part of their diagnosis and what is expected for them, and what is sort of tracked in kids who have autism, is that they need a particular type of routine. There's safety in the routine and there's a particular type of comfort in the routine.

And I need that routine, too. I need that particular type of comfort. So that's home for me. And the understanding or the expectation that things will be as they are, I kind of like that. I like the expected. I don't like a whole lot of surprises.

Tahat

It's funny because we started the conversation with you talking about, you know, being in the country of Eastern Oregon. Not having a sense of community. I think that's an interesting place to think, too, about your role with Kundiman, and your role as a community builder. Is there a relationship between having had a lack of community, and the role that you see yourself in now and how that feels like home to you?

de la Paz

If you ever have the chance to see what Kundiman does, I think that you know, the community that Sarah and Joseph have built over the years is really foundational for a lot of artists. One of the things that having a community that's like a home for folks does is that it grants them permission.

I think that in the Asian American community, in particular, there's a lot of trauma that isn't talked about. I mean, if we think about it, particularly the newer immigrants—say the Cambodians, the Vietnamese, the Hmong population—they're the children of war. And so the space that we provide in Kundiman, that Joseph and Sarah have been providing for years, has been a space that often allows people comfort, routine, ritual, all these things that we talked about. The expectations of home in the sense that you belong.

The other thing with the Asian American community is that sometimes, because we're sort of a newer immigrant population, there's a misunderstanding that resides in the artist. We don't understand the artist in the community. It's not practical. It is not something that say, first-generation immigrants expect from their children.

I also bought into that. And I think that as I've developed in the community, I've also found a particular type of home in that kind of work, in that kind of community building.

Tahat

One of my obsessions is the ethics of witness, and particularly in relationship with family. And *The Boy in the Labyrinth* is a deeply autobiographical book, about your two sons. But the actual poems have very few first-person pronouns, right? And the poems are very allegorical and mythic like we've talked about. The speaker is omniscient and often sort of disembodied. And I'm curious, as I think about the poetics of witness: the way to maintain a certain kind of ethic, at least for me, is to sort of have your body at stake. To be in it. And so I'm curious for you, how do you wrestle with the ethics of witness? With a disembodied voice?

de la Paz

That's a great question. I think that it is still something that I'm struggling with in this book. Gabby, you noted that there's sort of a preface that opens up the book, and I think that is functionally the place where I offer my body, but I don't offer it anywhere else in the book. And I think that's a conversation I'm still having with myself as I perform the work. I think what's particularly fraught for me as a neurotypical person is talking about issues of neurodiversity.

What I know is that the work is asynchronous with how I think and how I am now as a parent. And that's okay, right? That's okay that in my process of being a parent and being a poet and learning and growing from this process, I understand that there are moments where this mask is problematic. I mean, it is, and I have to own that. It doesn't mean that I don't love the work that I did and that I don't embrace it. But I have to acknowledge that there are moments when I'm worried that I might hurt my son, I might hurt my children, I might hurt somebody from the neurodiverse community.

I think that I'm attempting in the opening and in the closing to say, "look, I understand the limitations of myself as witness"—and I think that it's just a gesture, right? It's just a gesture. It's not going to solve everything. But it's more or less an assurance for myself that I'm trying to learn. I'm trying to do good. I also think that it's important to educate yourself. There's some really great work by neurodiverse artists out there. There's a series of chapbooks called Unrestricted Interest, and it's put together by Chris Martin. He basically publishes a lot of neurodiverse artists who are non-verbal, who are just amazing artists.

I really am trying to negotiate my positionality. I know it's fraught—I understand that. It's fraught. I understand that I'm vulnerable, that I'm liable to hurt people's feelings, but I think that part of my efforts to talk about it, including having this conversation, is to say, look, there's work that's being done by some really fantastic neurodiverse people. We should pay attention to that. We should really jump on board for that, for that wonderful work.

Tahat

I'm curious too about the choice to not name your sons in the book.

de la Paz

I had them named, and then I took it out. In several places they were named, and then I struck them. Part of that was editorial, there were just some inconsistencies. But another part of it was that I wanted at least the veil of protection. It's hard to write about family. It's really hard.

I did talk to them about this, that I was writing about them, but not for them. And I think that my oldest understood. He says, "I get it. It's fine." He may have a different answer at 16. He may have a different answer when he's 21. I have to acknowledge that we are, as people, in flux too. I have to respect his interest in his interiority. He also certainly understands where I'm coming from as a writer. He doesn't block me or prevent me from writing certain things. But again, he's still young, so that may change.

Hughes

I'm hearing that this book has taught you something about a poem as a gesture—and the intention behind just doing a poem, how that can sometimes fail, and taking ownership in "the failure of the gesture."

de la Paz

This book is entirely about failure. I think that it's important to say that it opens with an essay about failure. I understand that there are ways in which I'm not going to reach the community that I want to reach. That said, myth is one way to access or attempt to access a community.

Who has access to that community, a particular type of community? Who knows Theseus in the Minotaur myth? That's a particular community, right? And so immediately, because I'm using this allusion, I know that I'm not going to reach certain people. I know that I'm not going to reach my kids. I think that trying these particular types of skins is a way of stepping into different vehicles. Here's the tenor. I'm going to try different shapes to express that tenor in a way that maybe you'll understand.

There's a particular type of labor that happens between us when we're trying to understand, or when we're trying to negotiate the terms of our discussion.

Bates

You mentioned trying on skins, which made me think about the anthology that you edited, *A Face to Meet the Faces*, which is all about persona poetry. And that was years ago. But I'm wondering how you're thinking about persona poetry maybe differently now than you did when you were putting that anthology together.

de la Paz

Can we talk about Keats? I might get in trouble here. There's this idea that Keats grants you permission, the negative capability that you can inhabit all these selves. That you can aspire to write. It's this particular type of permission. I don't know if that works in this era. You know what I mean? I don't know if that works without a particular type of informed consent, if that makes sense. There has to be some level of understanding.

I think it's the same understanding I had when I developed the anthology with [my co-editor] Stacey Lynn Brown. There's a particular boundary, a particular type of negotiation that you have to do when you're trying on a face. And then you're trying on a skin.

There are two things that you've got to consider when you're thinking about persona. You're thinking about accuracy, conveying this person accurately. But then you also have to think about whether you're attuning yourself to that particular persona. And attunement is kind of the bigger, broader category of—"Have I read and understood the history? Have I looked at that community and understood the community in my limited capacity? What are the boundaries of territory that I can't cross? So, if we're juggling these two ideas, accuracy and attunement, I think in a lot of ways attunement and centering yourself and the skin is far more important.

Tahat

I'm curious about failure. I think it's really interesting to propose that this book is about failure. And I think, I guess we're probably being honest, a lot of us start writing poems from a place of failure, but never get to that self-realization. As a matter of craft, how do you then know that your poem isn't a failure?

de la Paz

I ask my students this: "How do you know when a poem is done right at home?" I just send them out. Sometimes I let someone else make that decision and then I come back to it, and then I renegotiate my relationship with the work. I always view publication not necessarily as an end, but a part of the editorial process. I think that's a healthy way to think about publication, right? Sometimes you just have to surrender the work. Sometimes you have to let it go. I'm very much in process. I'm thinking about this book, and how I think about it is constantly changing. Robert Lowell was constantly revising his work. I'm still noodling and taking out words as I read.

But in a lot of ways, performance—when you perform the work—that's a different type of revision, right? You're changing the work so that it performs well in front of a particular audience. You're changing the way in which the art occupies a space. Certain poems aren't going to work as rendered, so you have to change them. And I think that that's okay. That's part of the process.

Hughes

I mean, isn't every poem a failure in a way? Every poem is somewhat of a gesture, and a gesture is just leaning towards the actual thing. In some ways, poems are… it's the closest sort of thing to what you want it to be, but it's still not going to be done. Everything's a failure.

Bates

I mean, we're getting into some philosophical conversations now. But the language itself is a failure. And therefore, how can poetry, which is the art of language, not also be a failure?

de la Paz

I think that part of the thing that we're negotiating with is we're trying to represent—in our best way and in our best space at this particular time or this particular moment—an emotion or a belief or a feeling. And you're not going to feel that ten minutes later, you're not going to feel that an hour later, but someone else might.

And that's the negotiation of art, right? You create this thing and then you move on, because your feelings and your moments and your being is asynchronous with the art that you've made, but it might be synchronous with someone else.

Monuments for Men (Memory's Vault), Fort Worden

Shin Yu Pai

for Courtney Hudak

I can't deny that beauty is
here, when bullied by design

to turn my back to the bay
and enthrone myself beneath

the shelter, to sit opposite a single
pale stone, enshrined inside a slab

mausoleum—the permanence
of rock is as persistent as the force

of men, it's evident in the words
etched onto stone steles, hostile

architectures crafted by those
who saw themselves like gods

who coerced the eyes upward
to poles planted at the site,

that old trope of the man, &
his lover the sea, patiently waiting

for his return, I think why
not turn the gaze back on her

right now—the sea—we have
already seen all there is to see

A La Fuerza

María de Lourdes Victoria

Ahora por fin comprendo, a mis sesenta y tres años, que mi padre estaba equivocado cuando decía: "A la fuerza ni los zapatos entran, m'hija". Así me advertía de niña, arrullándome en la hamaca, a la sombra del framboyán, al caer la noche. Cansado, tras haberle "dado a la caña" todo el día—a esa mata ingrata que lo doblegaba, quebrándole la espalda y los sueños—a cambio de un puñado de frijoles, ahí, al vaivén de esa hamaca me aconsejaba, a la hora del zancudo.

Hoy, todavía alcanzo a oír su voz gangosa, curtida por tanto aguardiente y tabaco, que al final, de nada le sirvieron: ni uno ni el otro lograron sosegar sus tristezas. "A la fuerza ni los zapatos entran, m'hija", susurraba y yo, esa niña que cabeceaba en sus brazos, se lo creía.

Se lo creí hasta los trece años, hasta ese día infame que me llevó a la ciudad y me entregó a aquella familia de ricos, porque después de todo, ya era hora de que me ganara la vida, y porque, además, "aquí no te va a faltar nada, m'hija, aprovecha lo que bien te den estas gentes; ya sabes que a la fuerza…" "Ni los zapatos entran," completé el dicho, porque la voz ya le carraspeaba y los ojos se le inundaban de lluvia. Prometí echarle ganas a mi nueva vida aunque nada me faltaba, que no fuera su olor a humo y a tierra mojada.

Como fue, en esa casa de ricos todo sí entraba. A la fuerza. Los gritos de la doña entraron por no espulgar bien las lentejas, por no desmanchar las pantaletas, por lavar mal los platos y hablar así, como india de rancho. Entraron los empujones de la cocinera, por estorbarle en la cocina, por desordenarle la despensa y por andar de metiche, espiándola, cuando se besuqueaba con el jardinero. Los pellizcos de las hijas malcriadas entraron también, sin censura, por no haberles tendido la cama, por no haberles hecho bien las trenzas o nada más porque no tenían qué hacer y andaban aburridas.

El patrón entró a mi cuarto un día, sin tocar la puerta. Entró borracho y vehemente a enseñarme que, a la fuerza, todo sí que entra, ¡claro que entra! Con un solo empujón y con un par de cachetadas. A la fuerza, hasta los zapatos entran. Hasta la zapatilla de la Cenicienta le entra a una india pata-rajada y coqueta, como yo. Y de nada sirve ponerse terca. Más vale cerrar los ojos y aflojar el cuerpo. Lo mejor es aflojarlo todo, sobre todo la conciencia.

Quise hacerle ver su error a mi padre. Viajé descalza, sobre suelas encalladas, hasta mi pueblo, pero llegué tarde. En la hamaca, bajo la sombra del framboyán, lo esperé hasta que cayó la noche. Lo esperé esa noche y muchas otras. Lo esperé hasta que cayeron todas las noches, de golpe, sobre mi cuerpo quebrado. Cuando comenzó la quema, corrí por el manto de cenizas, hurgando los escombros del desierto. Volqué piedras, rascando las cicatrices del fuego, removiendo raíces calcinadas, sin encontrarlo. El rumor empolvado que ceñía mis huellas juró haberlo visto, muerto en algún barranco. Se lo llevó la caña—y el trago—me dijo. Se lo llevaron a la fuerza, pataleando.

Viajé descalza, una vez más, sobre mis suelas chamuscadas, rumbo al Norte, rastreando aquel puñado de frijoles que tanto eludió a mi padre. Crucé cerros, ríos y fronteras, caminé resuelta, sin más escudo que mi cuerpo taladrado, mismo que con tanta pericia supo filtrar desdichas y esquivar contratiempos. Así pues, llegué intacta al otro lado. Al lado de los valles irrigados. Al huerto de la abundancia. Fue entonces que yo, la mujer perforada, le exigí todo a la vida.

Sí se puede, a huevo que se puede, ha sido mi lema. Con los ojos cerrados y la conciencia inerte, pero lúcida, he logrado mi quincena, mi techo de ladrillos, una alacena llena y una pila de hijos, y de nietos, que nunca he tenido que regalar a nadie. Toda una vida 'le di a la manzana'—fruta ingrata que me ha dejado la espalda encorvada pero mis sueños erectos. Y hoy, por mucho que me aprisionen estas rejas artificiales, nada detiene mi esencia agujereada. Como arena en coladera, mi vejez se desliza por las rendijas. Ando libre, a mis anchas, por los campos fértiles. Camino descalzo, como una Cenicienta morena, oliendo a humo y a tierra mojada que día tras día retomo, con este puño artrítico, a la fuerza.

de Lourdes Victoria

Crayfish in Pond at Mount St. Helens.
USDA Forest Service, Pacific Northwest Research Station, 2018.

The Bubble
Max Delsohn

> "Why do you play such dreary music on Saturday afternoon, when tired
> mortally tired I long for a little reminder of immortal energy?"
> —Frank O'Hara

On the first sunny day of the season, the city of Seattle went to Cal Anderson Park. It wore shorts, tank tops, bikinis, flip flops, sun hats, and cutoff overalls; it lounged on beach towels, jumped for frisbees, clustered under Red Maples, crouched to pet French Bulldogs slobbering exuberantly. It shouted and smiled with alien urgency, and every breath it took seemed to crackle with potential. On the first sunny day of the season, the city of Seattle remembered it was alive.

Like everyone else, I had come to the park in my Sunday best—crisp black muscle tank and salmon pink chino shorts—to see if the warm weather would solve all our problems. What might Seattle become beneath the sun's luscious yellow spell? Especially here were queers, most of whom I'd seen before, but that was to be expected. We weren't a small community but there were only so many protests, so many independent bookstores and gay bars. Maybe today would be the day we'd all finally fuck in the grass or bathe naked in the fountain, do something—anything—that broke up the usual rainy, gentrified monotony. Yes, the whole city of Seattle was outside today, but we were the main attractions, the stars of the show, hot for disruption and cruising for newness.

It was in the midst of such fantasizing that I found Hunson, inconsolable, on a hot patch of turf in the park. He looked more glamorous than ever. His Lululemon clad legs stretched out before him, and his peroxide blonde hair blazed with sunlight. Beneath his Ray-Bans, I could tell he had shut his eyes. He looked as if he were in pain.

"I can't believe she's done this to me—THEY, oh my god, they."

I squinted at my friend and asked what he meant. He peered around suspiciously, like he feared being caught with a terrible secret.

"It's Miranda," he said. "She's a they now. She is *they-ing out*." Then he spit on the turf, which did not absorb his saliva at all but seemed to showcase it in its slow, grotesque bubbling.

"Since when?"

"Since LAST TUESDAY. Since longer! Since forever! You know how these people are. *I was really a boy all along* or some such crap."

I laughed a little. "Isn't that what you said when you came out, too?"

"How dare you compare me to her," Hunson said gravely. He produced a bubble tea from his purse and sipped from the fat, white straw. "Sorry. To *they*."

"What's their name?" I said.

"Dayton," Hunson said. "You know, like the city in Ohio."

"Yikes," I said. Hunson threw his head back and cackled.

"I know, right? Third name's the charm, sad sack! Who told this *sad sack* that naming themselves 'Dayton' was a good idea? Where are the gatekeepers when you need them?"

"All right, all right," I said. Even for Hunson, this was getting a bit much. "Let's be discreet in our deadnaming of enbys."

"Ugh," Hunson said, taking another loud slurp of bubble tea. "Always hated that term. Enby enby enby. It's so cutesy. I bet Dayton fucking loves calling themselves an enby."

"Hunson, easy!" I cried. My volume surprised us both. Clusters of people around the park had turned to look at us. Then Hunson stood up and put his hands flat on my chest. He'd done it every time I'd seen him since I'd gotten surgery.

"Darling, is this about the time I accidentally called you *Joy* without knowing... well, you know," Hunson said. "I was just trying to say you made me happy. If I had known that you were once literally *named*—"

"I don't..." I faltered. "I don't think you should resort to transphobia to make yourself feel better about a breakup. It's cruel."

Hunson pouted. He was mocking me.

"Trans people can't be transphobic, sweetie," he said as he picked up his purse and bubble tea. "Besides, you know I'm right."

I stood still, dumbfounded. Hunson was walking away.

"Right about what?" I called after him. "And yes they can!"

Troubled by this new development with Hunson, I began a lap around the whole of the park in an attempt to cool off. The turf field stopped at the baseball diamond; I cut through the dirt there then walked the concrete path between the dugouts and the basketball courts, where men were playing a lively shirts vs. skins style pickup game. Then I walked past the bathrooms and onto the real grass that covered the larger, north end of the park.

On a small hill towards the back of the park, I saw my friends Denae, Marshall and Abigail arranged in a circle with their backs pressed against each other, as if they were keeping watch. Denae saw me first. They had been marveling at a French Bulldog leaping for a tennis ball before spotting me on the grass below.

"Our friend! Our friend!" Denae cried. I remembered, then, that they had posted a tweet that morning about 'vibing with Lucy 🌀.'

Marshall and Abigail turned to face me. They started chanting along with Denae: *Friend! Friend! Friend! Friend!*

I waved and walked to the top of the hill. I tried to forget about

Hunson and hold onto that vague, shimmering hope as Denae and Marshall made room for me to join the circle.

"Add your back to the core," Denae said. "We're so much more powerful with you here."

"Good," I said. "How's the trip going?"

"Is it that obvious?" Marshall said as he leaned his head into mine.

"Relax, Marsh," Abigail said. Her ponytail brushed against mine. "It's Cal Anderson. Nobody cares."

"This shit is good. Really good," Denae said. Their moved their hands over their neck as if it were a lover's. "Barry hooked it up."

"Who's Barry?" I asked.

"He's my ex, like ancient ex," Abigail said. "He grew up here so he has a lot of connections."

"When we went to pick up, we realized I'd fucked him too, like last week!" Marshall said, grinning hysterically. "Barry gets around! Good job Barry."

"How was he in bed, anyway?" Abigail said.

"Mediocre," Marshall said. "Too much eye contact."

My mind flashed, briefly, to a man I had seen a month or so before. We'd met through Grindr—he hadn't had a username, but when I entered his apartment, I'd seen a piece of mail addressed to Barry Mercer. He'd had a kitchen scale on the desk in his bedroom and made too much eye contact. But because of Marshall and Abigail's history, I did not mention this, as it seemed some sort of equilibrium between them had been reached.

"How's your trip going?" Denae asked me.

"I'm not tripping right now," I said. "Just soaking up the sunshine."

"What's wrong?" Denae asked. I hadn't wanted to talk about it, but Denae always knew.

"I just had an odd exchange with Hunson. He's freaking out about Dayton. Did you three hear about Dayton?"

"Who's Dayton?" Denae said. "Never heard of him."

"It's they," Abigail said. "You know Dayton. Hunson's last partner."

"Oh shit, Mir—yeah!" Denae said. "They transitioned? Didn't see that one coming at all!"

"Neither did Hunson," I said.

"I'm not super surprised," Marshall said. "They always had a kind of twink sensibility. Sort of twee twink. Folk twink? I mean who owns *that* many gingham dresses?"

"True, babe," Abigail said. "But aren't they dating a girl now?"

"Yep. Amazon simp, one of those *queers who code*, total snoozefest," Marshall said.

"Oh, so that's what this is about," said Denae.

"What is?"

"Hunson's having a crisis of masculinity."

"Totally," Abigail said. I could hear the sharp flicker of a lighter, then a long inhale. "He invested his entire gender identity into their masc-femme dynamic. If Dayton's not a femme—never *was* a femme—then what does that make Hunson? Back then and now?"

At this Denae turned. "You know, for a straight girl, you're weirdly queer-competent."

Abigail took another hit from her joint. "I just listen. Plus all of my friends are gay. Even my ex-boyfriend is gay." She gestured to Marshal, who shook his hair and whinnied like a horse.

"Maybe there's a reason for that," Denae said with a shrug. Abigail snorted, and Marshall gave me a look that said *she's totally into Denae*, and the troubled feeling inside me dissipated. Marshall's eyes flashed with genuine enthusiasm. He was happy for them; it made him look older, somehow.

We sat in the easy quiet at the top of the hill for some time. We talked about our bad service jobs and latest crushes and the ongoing gentrification of the Hill, like the condos that now loomed on all edges of the park, casting unnatural square shadows on the grass and trees, and how nobody knew how to stop it. Then, somehow, the conversation circled back to Hunson. My troubled feeling returned.

"Sometimes I think Hunson forgot he's trans," I said.

"It's like all Hunson *is* is trans," Denae said. "Like he's the Adam of trans guys and every other transition is in reference to his. He's always had weird stuff about enbys. If you told me he ran one of those truscum Tumblrs in undergrad, I wouldn't bat an eye."

"Pretty self-absorbed," Abigail said. "It must have been really hard for Dayton to come out on the heels of a breakup with a trans guy who has that many followers on Instagram."

"Nothing makes me want to detransition more than Hunson's Instagram," I said.

"Why are you even friends with that guy?" Abigail asked.

"Everybody's friends with Hunson," I said. "He's Hunson."

"I don't get it." Abigail said.

I tensed up and braced to defend my position. But Denae, happily under the influence of their crush and of LSD, responded more honestly on our behalf:

"How many trans people do you think there are in this city? In the world?" they said. "We're a minority within a minority. We try to be a family. We have to try. Hunson's like our beautiful, colicky nephew who smears his shit on the crib. If we don't change his diaper, who will?"

At this, all four of us laughed, and I was glad that nobody spoke further. We looked out onto the throngs of people in the park. More of Seattle had arrived. Some were drinking from brown paper bags; others were openly downing PBRs and cans of wine. The robust goodwill of the morning had begun to morph into something hot and frenzied, lustful and raw.

Over by the fountain stood Tyler, another trans guy who often needed his proverbial diaper changed. I suspected he and Hunson had been fucking again, due to a particular density of fire emojis from Hunson on Tyler's most recent selfies. He saw me looking and waved me over. I kissed Denae on the center of their forehead, said goodbye to Abigail and Marshall, and walked in Tyler's direction.

Tyler stood alone on the concrete, shirtless, dipping his fingers into the fountain's clear water. His top surgery scars blended seamlessly into his sculpted pectorals; abs rippled across his stomach and a sprig of pubic hair poked out of the front of his low-rise jeans. He'd cropped his black curls short and even seemed a little taller. I stole a look at his shoes to confirm; yes, there under his jeans were the same high-tops I'd order from TallMenShoes.com, back when I was beginning a transition of my own. The last time I had seen Tyler was outside of The Rendezvous, where he had tried to pay me a dollar for a cigarette, even though I'd already told him several times that night I'd quit smoking the previous year.

Once I arrived, Tyler pulled me in for a hug. His skin was warm from the sun and bizarrely soft. Guys this pretty always moisturize.

"Been forever, big man! *Love* the long hair. Seems like the whole city's out today—Speaking of, you see any Hunsons jerking their jerk selves around here?"

I told him I'd just run into Hunson an hour or so before.

"He's texting me a ton," Tyler said. "Totally freaked over Dayton. You hear about that yet?"

I told him that I had.

"So weird. Hunson and I hooked up before *I* transitioned. Was all for me starting T. He even put in a good word with Dr. Rolfe so I could skip the new patient wait list. Sweet as a rhubarb pie."

"Huh," I said. I myself had waited five months to get in to see Dr. Rolfe. And that was considered speedy. Hunson hadn't offered me the privilege.

"Maybe it's cause Hunson and I were never a couple," Tyler said. "Just two horny ships passing in the night."

"Not passing, then," I corrected.

Tyler frowned. "That's fucked up, man. I totally pass. I haven't been ma'amed since month three."

"Oh, no, that's not what I meant," I said. "You were saying about ships—"

"In fact I was passing at grocery stores and shit before hormones. I've been the manliest fag in this city for years, including you, buddy."

"Woah, woah," I said. "Your *metaphor* didn't make—"

"Hey baby girl, is this man bothering you?" interjected a man stumbling towards us. He was waving around a brown paper bag, spurting drops of liquor on the concrete. He was speaking directly to me.

Tyler raised his eyebrows but said nothing.

"Fuck this," I said, and started walking away.

"Respect your elders, girlie!" the man cried out. Tyler yelled something after me, too, but I was already gone. I marched into the grass and past a gaggle of toddlers to secure the last available swing on the playground across the park, far away from anyone who cared about passing or Dr. Rolfe or abs.

I did swing for a while. I pushed and pulled the chains and thrashed my feet until I lifted up into the sky. Then I relaxed into the momentum I'd made: the easy pump of my legs, the rusted creak of my back and forth, the sweat on my neck blown cold. The sun was lower now and in my eyes; it washed the park with gold light, Seattle blurred into silhouette, and Red Maples burned hot all around us. We were at that strange hour of afternoon when the world glowed gorgeous and perverse. I swung so hard that at my peak, my chains were parallel to the ground, and I was the highest person in the park, above the drinking and smoking and tripping and flirting and eating and screaming, I was off the ground and lurching out of my body, out and above it all and gone, gone, gone.

When my breath grew heavy and remote, I stopped pumping my legs. I held tight to the chains and let myself pendulum freely until the tips of my sneakers dragged through the sand.

It was at this moment I realized there were no longer children on the playground—just an older lesbian couple with a stroller moving hastily away from the slide. They were fleeing from the adult moaning on the top of the play structure.

"Nobody knows the *trouble I've seen...*"

Hunson.

"Nobody knows my *sorrow...*"

I planted my feet firmly on the sand.

"Hunson!" I said. "What are you doing up there?"

"Who are you!" Hunson cried. He was lying on the platform face-up, but then turned his blonde-tufted head to look at me. "Oh, it's you. I already talked to you."

"You're scaring away the kids," I said as a mother and her two toddlers rushed hurriedly past. "Why don't you come down here so we can talk?"

"Down where?" Hunson said. At this he sat up. He had a miniature bottle of Fireball in his hand. He downed it in one gulp then took another out of his purse.

"Come on, Hunson. I'll share a Fireball with you."

"Everybody hates Fireball."

"Not me," I said. "Let's talk."

Hunson huffed. He made a big show of how laborious it was for him to stand up. He bowed. Then he sat down again so he could ride the slide down with his Fireball still in hand.

"Are you still upset about Dayton?" I asked when he arrived at the bottom.

"Gooooood work, Sherlock!" Hunson said. He offered me the half-full mini, which I swallowed hastily. I didn't really care for Fireball.

"I ran into Tyler earlier," I said. Hunson whipped his head around.

"Tyler? He's here? Where? That hot bastard hasn't responded to my texts all day."

"He was busy," I said. "Showing his abs off by the fountain."

Hunson dissolved into a dreamy, childlike swoon. "Those abs are really something, aren't they?"

"Why doesn't Tyler bother you?" I asked.

"Bother me?" Hunson said. "Does he think he's bothering me? More like I'm bothering *him*. I can't get the boy to shoot me a damn text!"

"No, I mean like the fact that he transitioned. He was out as a cis lesbian when you two first met."

"Oh," Hunson scoffed. "Tyler was always already a boy. He's the butchest thing this city's ever seen. I saw his transition coming a mile away. We were always two boys, *together*. God, that was back in my bottom phase. Never again. I'm waaaay too atrophied for that."

"So you're upset about Dayton because… you didn't predict their transition beforehand?"

"No!" Hunson said. He stuck his hand defensively in his purse. "I'm upset because Dayton's *copying me*."

I laughed. Hunson glared and pulled out another mini.

"I have proof. They're seeing Dr. Rolfe, my doctor."

"So is Tyler!"

"Because I got him in there. I get everyone in there. Unless you're Dayton and you don't come to me!"

"That isn't proof, Hunson. And you didn't get me in there."

"Well what about this—they got my same haircut from my same hairdresser."

"Who, Blazer? He's the only out FTM hairdresser in town and his salon's right next to Queenies. And half of Lex has your haircut." I gestured to his One Direction knock-off cut. Hunson stamped his feet.

"No, no, *no*, you don't understand. We dated for two years—"

"On and off."

"Yes, we dated for two years, on and off—and in those two years, they never mentioned transition once to me! We talked about how happy they were with me as their masc, her as my—THEY—as my femme. It was our sex, our dance, our banter, our clothes, our pet names, our sex, our… everything."

Hunson hung his head.

"You said sex twice," I said.

"Well I meant to!" Hunson cried, then finished his mini. "It was good sex. But she was thinking about being an enby the whole time."

He swallowed hard and watched a French Bulldog puppy trundle its way toward a dandelion.

"They won't even talk to me about it now," Hunson said with tears in his eyes. "They didn't want my help with coming out, my input, nothing. I'm nothing to them."

I sighed.

"How many of those minis have you had today?"

"One," Hunson said. "...teen."

"Eleven?!"

"They don't need me!"

I pulled out my phone as Hunson sobbed into his hands. I started to order him a Lyft—private, so he could not inflict himself on anyone else—but Hunson resumed his blubbering.

"Dayton's jealous. You're all just jealous! You basically copied me, too. Copier! Remember when you came out and we went to Value Village and you bought all the same kinds of clothes? Two flannels, two button-downs, two nasty pairs of khakis. I should never have bought those khakis, and you shouldn't have either! No originality! That's why I never got you into Dr. Rolfe—because I knew you'd copy my hormone dose and get all the same surgeries and look exactly like me!"

I looked up at Hunson and laughed in disbelief.

"You slippery little fuck," I said. Hunson held my gaze until I shoved my phone in my pocket and began to walk away.

"Yeah, get out of here!" Hunson cried. "Copy cat! Copy... copy *pussy!*"

As the sun began to set, I realized I hadn't eaten since breakfast, so I began walking back through the park, towards the baseball diamond and the turf and the cheap Mexican food place with the glass bottles of Coke that I liked. Raggedy pink and orange clouds tore across the sky. My stomach gurgled; I had gotten so caught up in Hunson's melodrama I had entirely neglected lunch.

The pink and oranges clouds were to blame, I thought. What did I *think* was going to happen at Cal today? What did I actually believe was possible? I was always destined to run into a soulless Barbie like Hunson and waste this precious daylight, because I was still in the same queer community with the same embarrassing fucking hang-ups. Seattle was still Seattle, and we were never, ever, ever going to stop talking about shit that didn't matter. Not even for the perfect sunset.

I arrived at the turf. On the soccer field in its center sat a dozen, giant inflatable spheres with clear, empty columns down the center. I stopped to watch as a group of people climbed into these bubbles so that only their legs were exposed. Once everyone was situated in their respective bubbles, they began playing a clumsy version of soccer. Players waddled down the field until they lost control of their bubbles and went rolling forward; others pursued the soccer ball at full speed from opposite directions and rebounded off each other before either foot could make contact.

Everyone in the bubbles had the same shirt on: a lime green tee with white lettering on the front. I could not read what the shirts said—the plastic of the bubbles warped the words—but I could tell it was a sort of organization or company they had in common. The whole thing reeked of team building.

My stomach roared, but I sat down anyway. I had never seen anything like this before. After so much predictable, pointless conversation, I needed a little novelty, even if it was, well, this.

The bubble ball players—mostly in their 40s and 50s, all white, all cis—seemed to be having a marvelous time. One woman tried to kick the ball but instead flew backward as if on a cartoon banana peel and landed on her bubble's back; she whooped with laughter until she burst into happy tears. One man, who had managed to keep a visor on inside his bubble, was taking the game very seriously. He had figured out how to maneuver his bubble more efficiently than the others, and how to lean to one side and crane his foot towards the ball before his opponents. When he scored the first goal of the game—a ball kicked from half field that trickled into the center of the net—he did a bubble body-slam with another man on his team and bellowed with abandon.

As the bubble soccer went on, more and more people began to gather on the sidelines. They brought their burritos, their ice creams, their brown paper bags of alcohol. I saw Denae, Abigail and Marshall on the other end of the turf; they were propped against the chain-link fence of a dugout, watching the game in awed silence.

It was then that I noticed Dayton, sitting alone and watching the game.

They were several feet away from me, far enough so that I could stare for a little while without them catching on. They sat on a picnic blanket littered with two tote bags, water bottles, Gatorades and cans of wine. Their hair was short and swept to the side, not unlike Hunson's, and they wore a muscle tank and chino shorts, not unlike mine. Their shorts showed off their leg hair, which looked thicker than it had in the past. Was Dayton on T? How did *they* jump Dr. Rolfe's wait list? As soon as I had this thought, I cursed myself for thinking it. Then Dayton turned in my direction to grab one of the cans of wine behind them. I jerked my face away.

Really, I hardly knew Dayton; they only knew who I was because Hunson and I were friends, plus the usual run-ins at Timbre Room or wherever else. Why should I care if Hunson deadnames them? Why should I stick up for some just-hatched enby? Why think about Dayton or Hunson or Tyler or *any* of these people for more than one miserable minute? Dayton only ever glared at me anyway, no doubt because of my continued association with Hunson after their breakup. If I got too drunk at the bar, they wouldn't help me find a ride home—they'd look on and laugh in judgment. Wouldn't Tyler do the same? Denae's 'trans family' speech was a pipe dream. Or it was one big family of babies. Just babies smearing shit all over each other and calling it 'community,' selfish, boring babies doomed to babyhood for life.

Somebody blew a whistle. First quarter over. The bubble soccer players shimmied out of their bubbles and visited the sidelines to hydrate. The woman who had whooped until she cried came over to Dayton. Dayton stood up, dusted off their flannel, and lifted the woman's face into a kiss, too soft and sensual for the moment. Then the woman grabbed Dayton by the hand and dragged them over to the bubble she had just exited.

"You gotta try the bubble real quick!" the woman shouted. "Before Jared sees!"

Dayton's eyes darted over to the man with the visor, who was now sitting in a lawn chair and bouncing a small child on his knee. Then Dayton gave the woman a mischievous raise of their eyebrow and jogged over to the bubble. They were still giggling as they wriggled their way inside.

But once surrounded by the bubble, Dayton stopped laughing. They only stood there, staring around at the rest of the park as we stared back at them, their thin body stiff, their hands at their sides. They scanned the various onlookers until their eyes locked with mine.

Dayton's hands flexed and their eyes grew wide. The whooping woman grew concerned. She turned to face the bubble.

"Who is that? Hunson?" the woman asked loudly. Dayton shook their head and began to explain, but they were interrupted by a terrible scream from the sidelines:

"Get out of there, tiny! You might get lost in there!"

It was Jared, the man with the visor. He was still holding the child but standing, now. He held a straight face for a moment, then burst out laughing. The rest of the bubble players laughed with him, including the whooping woman, who laughed loudest of all.

Dayton frantically clawed at the inside of the bubble to lift it off their body. They ran back to their spot on the picnic blanket and buried their face aggressively in their phone.

It was then I noticed that, spilling out of one of their tote bags, was a copy of *Stone Butch Blues*. I did not recognize the cover—it was different than my own deteriorating, awful copy. Theirs appeared to be a newer version; in fact I had never seen a copy of *Stone Butch Blues* so unmarked, so glossy.

It must have been Dayton's first time reading it. Their first time reading *Stone Butch Blues*.

I walked over to the picnic blanket and sat down. Dayton did a double take as I approached but did not speak. I clapped my hand on their back and whispered, "You getting much reading done?"

Dayton smiled and shook their head. I felt them lean back into my hand. Then they opened a can of wine and pushed it towards my face.

I made myself comfortable on the blanket, took the wine in both my hands and drank.

Streetcars on Fremont Bridge, 1936.
Engineering Department (Record Series 2613-07), Seattle Municipal Archives.

Prayer for TriMet Line 17
Jaye Nasir

Heaven is a fog, I know it,
I've bitten its earlobe,
lived in its grass stains, opened
the seam of the night, and

founds its insides hot
and pulsing. The animals
there all speaking in words
and the humans only

singing. Hell itself has histories,
libraries, due dates. So stop
optimizing your time, stop
advertising—if you're gonna lie

at least put your heart into it.
I'll only swallow what's
covered in blood. I'll only sleep,
dream, forget—suddenly

I'll remember, try to write
it down, bungle the cadence,
feel euphoric anyway.
Thinking on the bus, thinking

as I'm running late to my low
wage job, what a terrifying gift
to be wearing this body,
talking in this voice, carrying

this collection I call a self,
making jokes, singing between
my lips, my thighs. I'm ripe
for judgment, for forgetting,

I have days laid aside for
misery, a whole season called
night, as many fears as ever
but somehow they taste

different, like the hot copper
tang of blood. What I mean
is: now nobody can convince me
out of kissing my own chaos.

You can't eat numbers,
they're icy cold, whereas
the night rolling by through
yellow light against glass,

man yelling at himself a row
behind me, the glowing black
eyes of my reflection—
all of this is alive and burning.

Dome in Camp Long, circa 1950s.
Ben Evans Recreation Program (Record Series 5801-02), Seattle Municipal Archives.

Cabin Life
Jennifer Fernandez

Back in the before-times, I used to preach online about the importance of a well-informed skincare routine. I'd rattle on explaining the differences between mineral and chemical sunscreens and the relevant benefits of hyaluronic acid and peptides to get that summertime dewy glow. I used to endorse cassava flour and collagen powder, maca, matcha, and fire cider for digestive health, and made money through corporate sponsorships, product endorsements, and giveaways. I was a lifestyle influencer hocking the virtues of living close to the land and nature, all from my cozy apartment in the city. Nature was a get-away, a place apart from the fermented funk of reality. But reality will find you even if you run away from it. Somehow it hitches a ride.

Everything falls into one of two categories, now: before or after. Before, picking dandelions was a novelty. A fun activity to do when my parents and I came out here for vacation. Gnarled roots for tea, bitter stems for sautéing, petals for salads. Now it's just another way to pass the warmer months. I've been here just over a year and a half. Or maybe closer to two years, now that I think about it. My last entry in here was two days before my twenty-seventh birthday. I gave myself the gift of not writing in this thing and now I've no clue what the date is. All I know is that there are long stretches of minutes behind me and an unknown number of days ahead. Starting this up again seems like a good idea, though. Another way to keep my mind busy. Look at me convincing myself that journaling improves one's quality of life. I've written whole posts on the subject!

My hope is that someday someone will happen upon this and find my story helpful. In that case, hello unfortunate person who finds my body! You'll have noticed that in earlier entries I kept things pretty light—the details of my Paleo breakfast, for instance. Re-reading them I'm embarrassed, writing as if I had an endless supply of paper but not saying anything. So this is my "Goals & Intentions" post (of sorts). When I'd do these online, my goals were things like "drink more water" or "be in nature more." I'd encourage followers to post their lists, tag me, follow the sponsoring product line, and comment. Giveaways could boost engagement, grow your followers, and produce user generated content.

So here are my Goals & Intentions for this journal: (1) Make it useful in some way to whoever finds this; (2) Write every day; (3) Be real!

—<o>—

He'd proposed his plan just before the rupture between before and after.

"If everything goes to shit and we need to leave town, we should go to your dad's cabin."

He said this as I was drifting off to sleep late one night. My mind exhausted from another day overrun by Zoom meetings, I thought I misheard him.

"Hmm? What??" I said, keeping my eyes closed.

"I just mean, things don't seem to be getting better."

My eyes smacked open. "What are you saying?"

He turned on his side, propping himself up on his elbow. "I'm saying that we can't wait until the world's on fire to come up with a plan. We need to start planning now."

There was a long pause and I could feel him deciding whether to continue. I lay still, doing my best not to interrupt his process. We'd been together long enough for me to know that if I attacked him with questions, he'd shut down. Finally, in the spiked tone he used when he needed to convince me of something, he started again, "I've been thinking about it and I think we need to have a bag packed, something light that we can just throw in the car in case we need to leave fast."

As much as I wanted to avoid sending him into a spiral, this seemed extreme to me. Things were bad, but I hadn't heard of anyone making exit plans. If they were, no one was talking about it. But it would make sense that we hadn't heard anything, since we made our plans in secret too.

There were sentiments surging, insidious and hateful. I figured they were fringe groups, people far away being stupid. And though we'd already weathered disapproving glances and infuriating comments from grandparents and uncles, I still had no clue how he felt or what he saw coming. I understand now that he could feel things in his body I couldn't, see things coming that I couldn't. Just by virtue of the body he lived in.

―◊―

On Tuesdays, or what might be Tuesdays, I gather firewood. I give myself about half the day to do this. It requires a lot of walking back and forth to and from the cabin, half the time lugging, you know, heavy stacks of wood. My own cottagecore CrossFit routine. The other half of the day, I like to work on something artsy or mellow like watercolors. I used to enjoy reading, but we didn't think to pack books. The only ones already in the cabin were a book on fly fishing and an old cookbook.

Mom brought the watercolors to the cabin years ago. She had an irritating habit of getting excited about a craft or activity, and then quickly losing interest and moving on to the next one. Before watercolors was aromatherapy, after watercolors was DIY tea blends, and then sashiko, the Japanese art of functional decorative embroidery. Each activity was something she'd learned about during book club or online. "Your friend Mabel has been talking about calligraphy meditation for days! How have you not heard of this?" Mabel was not my friend. I didn't even know her personally.

She was just another influencer who was probably making money off the calligraphy brush people. Mom was convinced we all knew each other and had brunch on weekends.

The summer she brought the watercolors to the cabin, she and dad were getting along surprisingly well. They'd been growing cold of late, each seeming to hide something from the other. I had put up a fight in the days leading up to that cabin trip, but honestly once we were here, it was nice to just watch them be kind to each other again. Mom made her "famous" pesto pasta—with extra bacon for me—and showed me how to use the watercolors by the light of the lantern. We sat and ate pasta and painted spindly flowers, saw-toothed leaves, and knotty trees. She hummed Jim Croce and the lantern gave off just enough light for us to tell the difference between indigo and black. Those cabin trips seem precious now—gardening, foraging, fishing, building fires. All those times I thought she was being flighty, distracted with new projects, or when I thought he was being obstinate, insisting that I go fishing with him or learn to cut firewood—they were really teaching me about the strange enchantment that exists between humans and nature. That alchemy between us. Maybe that's giving them too much credit, but I suppose that's how I understand it now that I've lived out here alone. Either way, I'm grateful. I'm grateful too that he got to know this place and my parents.

He'd met them once before at a dinner, but bringing him to the cabin was obviously a much bigger deal. I wasn't too worried. He was confident and beautiful. My parents loved him because he loved me. But he was easy to love. Some evenings we'd walk, just the two of us, out to the far end of the meadow. One night we stood under one of the trees silently surveying. He stood behind me and pulled me close, wrapping his arms over my chest. My back pressed up against him I could feel his heart beating, his breath on my hair.

—◆—

These days, I'm up well before the sun is above the mountains. But the honey glow of morning is only beautiful if you don't think about what might be happening on the other side of those hills. The other day, I had a dream that made me realize I still haven't written anything about what brought me here. But if I'm being truthful, I haven't been very truthful at all. I've been hiding from you. Maybe that's the real reason I haven't written in what seems like over a month.

In my dream I was facing the meadow, the sky burning and grainy as if it were made of a million fire ants skittering around. It throbbed and flickered, combusting and releasing back to earth all the crap we'd sent up, our bloated sentimentality, our misery, our pollution. My hands felt warm and wet. Blood streamed off my palms and dripped down my fingers. Garter snakes like moldy sesame noodles, twisted and curled around my feet. Crows swirled above me cawing. I woke up crying.

The night it happened we were fully asleep. Earlier in the evening while he was cooking dinner, he said he was sure some people at the store had been talking about him. By that point the car had been packed for a month. He'd been carrying supplies out to the trunk little by little in the middle of the night, in case anyone was watching. I thought he was being paranoid but speaking up at that point would have been absurd, so I just sat there, finishing my drink and listening. When he was done I walked over, put an arm over each of his shoulders, and got up on my tip toes. I kissed him and told him how "hard" it all sounded. I was an idiot.

We cleaned up the dinner dishes together that night like we did every night and he asked how my day had gone. I told him about the brand I was working with, which was a maker of ethical pet clothing.

"What's that? Like clothes that aren't uncomfortable for your pet?"

"No," I chuckled, "like not sweatshop made."

We talked about fast fashion, unions, and worker's rights. He washed, I dried. I didn't mention that earlier in the day my content manager told me she'd noticed an uptick of hits on a few posts featuring us as a couple. An anniversary post where I glowed about how happy I was we were still together, a vacation picture we took a couple years earlier in Burma. It never occurred to me to say something. As we went to bed, everything seemed as normal as was possible at the time.

There was a boom and a crash. Everything shook. In the dark a rush of bodies came into the bedroom. There was screaming and yelling coming from every single body. He shouted at me to run. So I did. But they weren't after me.

I drove close to 5 hours without stopping. When I arrived, I did everything as he'd planned. I blocked the path, covered the car, and walked the rest of the way, making sure to go through the rocks, I did all of it, everything. Just like he said. When the front door closed, it finally hit me:

I was here. He wasn't.

―◊―

After I arrived, I didn't know what to do with myself, so I tried to fill every second with activity. I saw once on a survivalist show that your brain needs things to work on so you don't go crazy in extreme isolation. It felt strange and uncomfortable not having anyone to talk to, no internet to post on, no friends or neighbors or strangers. I noticed that I'd started talking to myself, and that seemed weird so I started talking to the crows instead, which I thought was marginally better. Soon it dawned on me that before coming here I was surrounded by an endless barrage of stimulus. People talking at me online, comments and DMs, Zoom meetings, phone calls. There was always noise. Out on the street, noise. Watching videos on my laptop, noise. I thought I knew what quiet was, but it wasn't until I got here that I realized I'd never had quiet.

Even when we came here as a family, we'd have each other to listen to. Mom would hum while she worked on some project and Dad's newspaper would rustle or he'd be out cutting wood. There was always some other human making sound. But real quiet, the kind that exists when we're all too busy clamoring around, is like a vortex that can suck you up.

The total darkness of nighttime left me with nothing to do but stew in my own guilt and loneliness. In the beginning, I cried into the cabin's musty, overstuffed feather pillows, confronted by the vast silent ache of time and uncertainty before me. I had to get used to being alone during the day. I started writing in this thing again. I talked to the crows, gathered firewood. I learned to tend the garden, pick the elderflower, yarrow, and chamomile regularly. Botanical supports not only promote gut health, they can also be immunity and mood boosters. Now, I still fill my time, but more slowly, with purpose instead of desperation. Repairs are needed from time to time—a hole in the roof, a clog in the woodstove. But there isn't a night though when I don't think of him and of what I did.

—<o>—

The creek is about four miles away so I check carefully to make sure I have everything I need before leaving. There were a couple of times early on when I'd get to the creek and realize I'd forgotten the flies or the gun, so I'd either have to walk all the way back or just say fuck it, and leave everything to chance. Dad loved fishing and when we'd go out to the creek, he'd show me all his new ties. He wasn't so fancy that he'd make them himself, he'd buy them at the store, but he was always proud and excited to show me. I remember loving their brightness and flare. He'd tell me the names of each one and what made it special, but I just thought they were pretty and would look nice on a hat.

Today I used the long green and white tie, the one with a red bead for an eye. It dove deep down into a hole where the fish were and snagged one. That shocking snap and pull is always a relief. I was terrible at first, rusty from years of begging off whenever my dad suggested we go fishing.

Memo to whoever finds this: when packing your bug-out bag, make sure to pack yourself a lipstick. I know, you're probably thinking, "Who is she trying to look nice for? The crows?" But one day you'll wonder what your friends are up to and whether they're safe. You'll wonder if they've thought about you and whether they miss you too. You'll remember mimosas on Sundays, picnics and barbecues, birthday parties, and asking one another if you have anything stuck in your teeth. You'll miss laughing with them and then you'll cry praying they're not alone, like you. You'll want to look good for them, for the memory of them, in honor of them. There will be a day when you wish you could pretend, even for a little bit, like you're getting ready to meet them for coffee. You'll want to cover up your dry, cracked lips. Pack a lipstick. And if you can, try to make sure it's free of synthetic antioxidants like Butylated Hydroxytoluene which is known to cause liver damage. But honestly, who gives a shit at this point?

―◇―

The wind has been howling and whipping and I'm afraid if I go out there, I'll flake off into tiny pieces and be blown away like ash. I haven't left the cabin in over a week, I think. Today I watched as part of the fence got knocked over and dragged out to the meadow. An invisible hand took hold of it and, in a rage, twisted and warped it before sending it flying. Windstorms make me wish I could leave, get in the car and go, but I know it probably wouldn't start. Even if I did get it running, I have no way of knowing what I'd be driving back to.

Thick and heavy, I feel like I'm covered in moss or fur. Dank and woolly. My hands have become hooves, awkward and clunky. My teeth are loose. The wind keeps me up at night, but so do my dreams. Lying in my parents' bed I smell the pillowcases trying to find one last hint of their smell, but they hadn't been here for years even before I arrived. One took a long and arduous road to death, while the other went quick, as though by shortcut. They'd done their parts to make everything easy for me. Wills had been written, preferences stated, coffins and plots paid for. The only thing I needed to do was cry and grieve and wail. And I'd wanted to. But somehow I couldn't.

―◇―

The sun is out and the mountains are glowing, massive and plump. On these days, before the sun is high, the sky is the palest of pinks. Halfway up the hillside, mist lingers, slow and melty. The tops of the hills are a dark seaweed green, sandwiched between the milky blush of sky and the wispy mist that eventually slips away to some unknown place. I think we're all happy to see the sun again, the crows and me. It's been good to leave the cabin, check on things, look for that piece of ravaged fence. It's slow going. For the most part, things held up well. There's a lot to clean up but none of it is beyond repair.

A crow has been cawing out an alarm for days. I suspect there's something in the area like an eagle or owl. Usually they call out like that when there's something in their space that shouldn't be. I saw them once gang up on eagle ten times their size. They dive-bombed it, taking turns mobbing in and out. Eagles may be majestic, but the crows are scrappy, so I root for them. They come by and watch me when I'm outside and we talk. I tell them everything I can remember about him, like how he liked soft custardy scrambled eggs on Sunday mornings or how he'd stretch out long, like a cat in a sunbeam. With his hands way up above his head, he'd point his toes and extend his legs taut, making them look like pencils. His eyelids scrunched like walnuts. I used to watch him do this from across the room, admiring his sinewy muscles, the crack and snap of his ankles, the way his t-shirt would ride up and show the hair around his belly button.

—◇—

These days my body isn't up for the kind of work I used to do. It seems I'm always tired. One morning, I'd been out plodding in the garden for a bit but got hungry and could feel my energy waning. Standing to come inside, I glanced up at a crow who'd been perched on the fence watching me work—and then noticed behind him, just at the far edge of the meadow, a man standing under one of the trees. I don't know how long he'd been there.

I backed away and ran inside, going straight for dad's gun. My chest ached, my hands were sweaty and hot. All this time, and I'd never seen anyone. Who would even find this place? Why is he just standing there?

When I gathered the courage to peek out again, he was gone. Fear was coursing through my chest, but what struck me in that moment, what stopped me cold, was that he looked just like him.

―◇―

I packed a bag with some essentials and came out to look for you a few days ago. I know it was you that I saw. "Essentials" now boil down to a knife, gun, some bits of food, and my coat. A piece of paper, a pencil, and a needle and thread are my luxuries. You're out here. Maybe lost and hungry. My body is cracked and brittle and my gums are bleeding. I'm out further than I've been before but I can't leave you again. I can't see you, but you're there. Behind the tree that's behind that tree.

Not knowing what became of you means you're everywhere, and nowhere. You might be dead, or, like in a fairy tale you're alive and waiting for me in a tiny cottage in the woods living a parallel life. Maybe the crows know you too. There is a vacuum in these woods that splits with every caw and each skittering squirrel and mouse. I listen for your voice, an echo, a vibration through the trees. Are you calling out to me? Are you there?

Still Living Things
David Naimon

Before the white skies. Rose. Before Ismit was born, when the skies were still blue. Rose. She seemed from then. The before. From that time. Someone from the past that he wanted in his future. Before the failed aerosol injection into the stratosphere and the too-good-to-be-true solar refractors, she seemed like a time traveler to Ismit. Not from now, though she was. But from before. From before the white skies. Blue.

Both Kavic and Ismit avoided the central campus. It touted itself as a social utopia, a meeting place for those pursuing both the lowly vocations and the exalted professions, both the applied, practical sciences and the haughty pure ones. But the reality of it kind of sucked. Even if they hadn't been alley kids, squatters, harvesters of precious metals from the innards of trashed personal electronics, even if Ismit and Kavic had been more respectable downsector shlubs they would've still hated the school snobbery and one-upmanship on display. But Ismit didn't have a choice. He had a mandated class to finish if he wanted to avoid another stint in juvie.

Fortunately recent weather blunted any upsector-downsector fashion differential at the college, allowing Ismit to duck in and out without too much shame or too much gagging. The city was on double alert. UVA/UVB levels had exceeded maximum limits for nearly three months despite the newly touted solar refractor. The typical acid drizzle during the city's winter inversions was alarmingly sulfurous this season and people were encouraged to keep thermal suits on when possible. And thankfully no matter how one accessorized a thermal suit they still looked pretty stupid on one and all, rich or poor.

It was on the Quad where he saw her. No, to be more accurate, *he* was on the Quad, loping a diagonal across its spongy vegetation while Rose walked unsteadily around its perimeter. He'd noticed her because, well, how couldn't you? She stepped out of the Bio-Sci building with a stack of *books* in her arms. Ismit assumed this was some kind of ironic gesture, an act so not cool it was cool. As if she were anticipating the vector of cool from a future vantage point. He'd dismissed her as another too-hip upsector girl, the books a twee affectation. But then she tripped, let out a plaintive "ah-eh-uh" and alternately blanched and blushed while the books clunked around her.

As the world slowed to a stupid stare, Ismit found himself on all fours, rooting around before her piezoelectric demi-boots with their false buckles. He gathered her books, looking up into her rosy face as he lifted them to her, one clunky chunk at a time. He felt conscious of himself doing this, aware of participating in something dumbly archetypal. He knew he was reenacting a gesture, a boy-meets-girl-via-book-retrieval romantic trope, a trope he'd only seen in Introduction to Film Studies, never in real life, but a trope that nevertheless seemed terribly unoriginal to him. Thus, Ismit felt a little ridiculous that his heart fluttered so earnestly against his breastbone as he met Rose's eyes for the first time. The power of countless boys before him, generations of boys retrieving these unwieldy info-devices of old, had won the day, animating Ismit with a feeling he hadn't felt before.

It soon became clear that Rose finished her work-study at the same time as Ismit raced to Remedial Thought. Ismit dreaded the court-mandated soul-numbing seminar (a consequence of taking the fall for Kavic's hacking into the schools' nanofossil exhibit) and was thrilled to be waylaid by a girl.

It wasn't long before Rose and Ismit were walking the Quad's periphery together each day.

"I'm not pro-sidewalk," Rose said on one of these walks. "But once the sidewalk is there, I just think it's a lesser evil to walk on it than on the grasses. On the still living things, you know?"

Perhaps Ismit should've taken this as a red flag. Perhaps Ismit should've nodded politely and hightailed it out of there, loping a defiant diagonal across the spongy green as he did. Instead Ismit nodded and smiled. And rather than allowing his foot to err from the path into the field of still living things, he leaned his shoulder into hers whenever a trolley rumbled by.

Kavic owed him. Owed him big time. He had no points to spare on his citizen chip, not with his mischief-hacks, his unpaid parking fines, his ticketless trolley-hopping. Ismit could take the hit for him and he did. Gladly. And in a weird way he had Kavic to thank because of it. If it weren't for court, and court-mandated Remedial Thought, he'd never have met her. But Rose herself was a problem. Ismit knew it. Or rather, he knew that Rose *would* be a problem for Kavic. That Rose was a problem for Kavic that hadn't happened yet. That Rose was something from the past coming fast into their future.

Ismit couldn't hide that she was upsector but he wouldn't mention the sidewalks, or the books, or the way she glittered the edges of her popliteal vents. Or he'd just never hear the end of it. But mostly he wanted to be a fifteen year-old man who had kissed. Not an alley kid hoping to. One who has already kissed, will kiss again soon, and who, when he does, will draw upon kissing experience, a large reservoir of kissing skills from past kisses, to be able to kiss at any moment. He didn't want to do it wrong in other words. Or for anyone to know he might.

He thought back to Introduction to Film Studies, to the time when people watched "films." *Film* seemed like such a wrong word. The filmy squeak between his body and his thermal suit, the film atop his bricks of fermented pea-protein, smelling them to make sure they were still good, the oozy gunk that filmed the gears on Rho's prosthetic feline leg. A film just didn't seem like the right place to look for kissing advice, to look at kissing, to look at people who have kissed so as to be a kisser and then someone who has kissed too. Plus, the skies looked fake. Colorized. Blue. Everything about it seemed unnatural.

But time, of its own accord, somehow pushed things together, even lips. The first time Ismit and Rose kissed, they stood beneath Rose's undersized mechanical umbrella near the Quad. The books—dry, gigantic and angular—emerging this way and that from Rose's arms, jabbed into Ismit as he pressed closer. He didn't tell her he'd never kissed before. Even Kavic didn't know. *Especially* Kavic.

Ismit closed his eyes as he leaned in and to his surprise he recalled a book-retrieval scene from a "film." The boy in question, a teen-ish kid like Ismit, wore a black and white checkered shirt with a skinny leather tie. His greased hair swelled and crested in a perfect sine wave. He gathered the girl and lowered her, lowering himself over her with authority. It was there the logistics got a little fuzzy for Ismit. The boy seemed to gather her lips inside his mouth, the top and the bottom, the thick chewy middle of them and the thin tapered corners. They all seemed to disappear in there. Yet somehow, impossibly, he seemed to be inside her mouth too, his tongue sweeping and searching as if for a last lick at the bottom of a jar a smidgen too tall.

He moved toward Rose's face with a mustered confidence, reached an arm around her hip and prepared to dip her downward.

Rose laughed and pushed against his chest to part their faces.

He'd been a little overzealous, Ismit thought, realizing he had captured part of her lower nostril with his open mouth. He steeled himself for ridicule.

"You look like a turkey vulture when you make that face," she said, tenderly.

Ismit forced a smile.

"Hold your helmet," she continued, righting herself. "I've got just the thing for this." She wiped her upper lip and nose against the angular collar of her suit and fished for something. A rivulet of winter rain titter-tattered on Ismit's outer shoulder as she did.

"Put this on," Rose said. Her lips pursed as she clicked opened a hinged orbinette. She ran her finger, the longest one, in tiny circles across the waxy black surface of its interior. Then the pad of that slender finger, warm and spongy, danced across Ismit's lips, carefully tracing their shape. His lips felt tingly, swollen and large as if they floated detached before him.

"Now, try it again," she said. "But think of it more as a search and listen than a trap and capture." Rose closed her eyes and waited.

Ismit hesitated. He watched Rose sway, her mind in her lips.

"Imagine," she whispered, eyes still closed. "Imagine you're transferring it carefully to my lips. That you can't let it get on my face. Just my lips."

Ismit searched and listened, searched and then listened. Listened somehow with his mouth as hers searched back. He wished he could distill and freeze-wrap that memory—their first successful kiss. This moment of kissing, yes. But also of just having been so. He wished he could protect it in time. Protect it from time. But it had already spoiled. Whenever he conjured it now it was inseparable from Kavic's response to its retelling:

"What the hell, Iz?" Kavic had said "What would it take to get you to run the other way? Open, oozing sores?"

"She…"

"A snaggle tooth? A wall-eye?"

Ismit regretted telling Kavic before the words had even left his mouth. But who else could he tell? And how long could anyone withstand Kavic's *and?-so?-well?* barrage?

Naimon • 129

"Diaper rash on her face?"

He'd have to spin it better.

"*I* was the one wearing the black lip stuff," Ismit said again, as if that were a good thing. "She's kinky, Kav. It was a game."

"Does she have to literally fire a flippin' warning flare straight at your dome to make you see? To make you get the hell out of there? '*Don't let it get on my face? Don't let it get on my face?*' Fuck that Iz. Like, what the Fuck?"

Ismit could see how crazy it looked—kissing with crazy rules, with any rules—but in the moment it wasn't that way. He didn't feel cowed or nut-cracked by her, just grateful she'd laid out a path on which, if he followed it, he could do nothing but succeed.

Succeeding wasn't what Ismit thought it would be like. Succeeding made Ismit miserable. He'd thought kissing would be like the giant python he'd read about in *The Daily Influence*, the one that, after engulfing an entire adult deer, was so large, was so full, that it diverted the river it fell fully across. It lay there for days, jaws blissfully unhinged, immobilized by an oversized satisfaction. But for Ismit, the more he got—nibbles, sidelong brushes, gusts of humid respiration— the more he wanted. Years of kiss-studies within a fully kissless existence and yet before he knew it the allure of notional kissing, and the pride and satisfaction of real kissing, real kissing done well, became 'just kissing.' The wanting grew louder than the getting. Or maybe the wanting was always loud and the getting so wonderfully soft and quiet in return. A reward for the wanting. That is, until the day Rose said "hup" and grabbed his paw before it slipped through the zip-portal in her undershield.

"I want it too," Rose said, pressing Ismit's palm against the heated crotch of her shield's front panel. And that's when, just then, she pulled out the two tiny egg-shaped devices, the two matching TipToes, powder pink and baby blue, wobbling together in her cupped palm.

"But I want us to embed before we do, Izzie," Rose continued. "I want us to find zero together first." Rose bit her lower lip in that way that drove him crazy. "Will you?"

Ismit had no choice but to call in his favor with Kavic. And his ask was a big one. He couldn't go to zero with Rose without him. He had less than a pocketful of kopçik and needed Kavic's help to harvest enough metal for more. But he also needed him to be nice. And to Kavic's credit he was. But the mood was quiet, thick with a somber silence as they scrabbled through the scree of discarded electronics and other trash that formed the city's most artificial topographic feature, this mound of scrap they called The Barrow.

Kavic now knew that Ismit had embedded. Which made his niceness all the more impressive. Nevertheless, Ismit tried to hide the little limp he still had from the procedure, the ache at the egg-shaped lump in the back of his ankle. But it didn't matter. It didn't matter if he was about to or just had. He looked over at Kavic, prying open the back of a perfectly functioning first generation ScootCommute 115 motor. And at everything between them. All the trash, the mainly upsector trash. The same trash that when people like Rose wore it or drove it or viewed it, Kavic and Ismit had built a friendship out of mocking. And now one of those very things, something no alley rat would ever own, was inside his body. He looked across all of it, feeling his ankle throb as he did and wondered, is this what it means to become an adult? To lose someone you loved the most?

Everything felt over. Everything new and old sucked into the overness of it all. He scrunched down into a self-made nest of electronics and looked up at the next hill over, a high point in the city, the neighborhood where Rose lived. He had to admit he liked trash. He liked cracking it open and popping out the rhodium plating, swapping it for kopçik, and trading kopçik for whatever he wanted. It felt like life, that flow. A flow he felt a part of. He wasn't like Kavic he realized. If every piece of upsector trash tossed on The Barrow lifted him that little bit higher, that little bit

Naimon • 131

closer to love, to the girl he loved, that was a good thing. He needed that sense of future.

Life had seemed so wonderfully simple that day at the embedment parlor. Living that day did, but not reliving it. Lying in parallel recumbent chairs, he did think of Kavic. That what he was doing was stupid, snobbish, even a little desperate. *Maybe it was, was and was.* He did hate those up-sector women too, the ones who declared their embedment-status through gelatinous apertures in the heels of their eco-booties, or worse, flashed their impact scores from the fenders on their solar-powered scooters. And those hipnik district girls, the vegans and freegans who tattooed dainty birds or cute little nests across the bumps in their ankles, trumpeting their moral purity, they were no better.

But when Rose explained her desire to Ismit, in her own winsome voice, with words shaped by her unbelievably lovely mouth, it all seemed so right to him. To strive to get their ecoimpact to zero, to reach that place where nothing was harmed by their daily actions, and at the height of their shared ecological lightfootedness to then couple *for reals*.

Rose and Ismit were instructed to pick a person-specific species-disincentivizer, one's most adored creature, the one you would least want to kill, as the TipToe's barometer of one's Personal Ecological Damage Assessment(PEDA). After a brief consideration of Tasmanian devils, Rose selected the duck-billed platypus.

"They lactate *and* lay eggs," she said. "They defy categorization."

"Yeah?" Ismit said, unsure of the significance of this but acutely aware of the baby blue egg now throbbing inside his ankle.

Rose curled her pointer fingers like claws and bared her incisors for Ismit.

"And they've got a venomous spur," she said.

It about slayed him.

"That's bad-ass," he said.

Unavailable—Error 27: Extinct Species. Choose Again.

"Told ya," Ismit said looking at the screen and back at his girl-platypus.

"Choose something real. Something *around*," Ismit said. "A crow or a squirrel or a mouse or something."

Rose stuck out her tongue. "Just because they're not around doesn't mean it wouldn't motivate me to minimize their deaths in the abstract."

In the end, she chose the pigeon ("they deserve more respect," Rose said), and Ismit the calico cat, in honor of his feral fur-ball, Rho.

Ismit looked now across the distance, across the arcing curve of crap that was his and Kavic's kingdom, at his quiet friend and his already amassed trove or treasures, at this same friend who was still there with him, even knowing it all now, and Ismit knew he should've been thinking just how unbelievably lucky he was.

Everything about Ismit's life was different now. He was leaping toward difference. But this was different than that. Every couple days he would walk to the lip around the central sunken greenway that separated the lumpy Barrow from the sharp terracing of The Brow. Today was the tenth time he had done so. Two squirrels scurried up the trunk of a nearby composite arboreal structure chasing each other as he walked and stopped, bent over, straightened up, and walked again. Ismit could still hear them twitter and chirp as they dashed across a lateral branch and disappeared into the dioxide trap, the thick nest of crystalline twigs above the greenway. Couples frolicked atop the vegetation below, their thermal suits only half closed. It felt like spring today, or at least the hope of it. And Ismit's hope, to recapture that free and easy feeling of books tumbling and books retrieved, felt like a lot of hard work.

For one, he could only afford a ridiculously outdated Biotarsal, a refurbished unit that was missing its shoe-adapted pouch that its tickertape sputtered into. So every fifteen minutes or so, when it read whatever it read in his TipToe, Ismit had to stop, bend down, and tear off what it had printed out. Otherwise he'd have a trail of paper dangling behind his foot. Usually he did this, depending upon how fast he walked, two or three, or sometimes even four times, before he reached the greenway, collecting these read-outs to look over after he talked to Rose. But looking ridiculous like this, looking really stupid, something he had never cared about before, that was the least of his problems.

Shortly after they embedded Rose had handed him one of her books and said "This is for you." She closed his eyes with her fingers, one by one. And then, before he knew it, she was searching and he was listening. He could feel the weight of the book in his hands and her hips pressing its bulk against his belly. "Keep them closed," she said, stepping back now. "Count back from twenty before you open them. Twenty, nineteen, eighteen… That's right."

He did what he was told. He counted the numbers. And when he opened his eyes Rose wasn't smiling and saying 'ta-da!' gesturing at the gift she had given him. She was gone. He looked down at the book. It wasn't wrapped and it had a drab and rough blue cover for such a breathless title: *Glorious Flight: The Heroic Life and Legacy of Cher Ami*. A single slate gray feather stuck out from one of its first pages. As he moved in the light, it flashed here and there a pastel pink, a dusky blue, an iridescent green. He opened the book and found a note. "It's about a pigeon!" it said simply. "Turn to page eleven." Ismit turned to page eleven and found another note. "One plus One" it was titled. "One minus One" it was subtitled. "I know it's going to be hard for us to be apart until we zero. Until we zero together. But I want us to talk a lot. A LOT until we do. Let's kiosk tomorrow at 5pm. I already miss you! R"

She had said it so matter-of-factly that Ismit was sure he must've forgotten them talking about it, this separation. But how could he have forgotten such a thing? Such a huge thing. Or perhaps it simply was how things were done upsector. That this was so par for the course in up-sector courtship rituals that she presumed he knew that embedding meant stepping back too. To be fair, Ismit was, on his own, feeling funny about showing up to hang out with Rose with his clunky Biotarsal boot spurting out data the whole time. And there was an honest-to-goodness romantic aspect to the separation and the waiting. But he also knew how this looked. How Kavic would see it.

It was under this long shadow, one that seemed both friendless and loveless, that he walked on this weirdly spring-like day for his tenth kiosk with Rose at the greenway. He found his favorite, the one with the best view of the sunken green down below and slid into the booth, pulling the console arm before him. His ankle clenched as the Biotarsal sputtered out some more data. He bent down and tore it off and held it atop the three other pieces he had accumulated since he left. His days, time itself really, were marked now by these visits, by his anticipation of them, and his thinking about them afterwards. To visit, visiting, having visited. But each visit was more and more fraught for Ismit. Rose had zeroed almost a month ago now, and each week his calico cat death eco-impact score hadn't budged one bit. Even with the humiliation of walking (with his obsolete tech) instead of trolleying it, even with him skipping out on his commute to school altogether.

He looked down at his stack of paper, tempted to look at the current output before he talked to Rose. But he wanted to be in a good mood. Remarkably, she had been. Whatever she was feeling about having a partner who couldn't seem to get his act together to even make the slightest progress, she didn't show anything but joy to see him. Each and every time. Ismit synched his credentials and there she was, already there, her pigeon avatar waiting for him. Rose rustled and fluffed up her feathers at seeing him, just the way he had grown to love. He slinked past her, rubbing his sleek furry body against her downy round form, circling her with friction, and then touching her beak with the tip of his tail. She nipped. They both laughed. They found a nice spot to curl up together. Half nest, half den by a small bubbling creek.

Of course, the predator-prey relationship between their two creatures became all the more obvious and comical in visual form. They had laughed about it the first couple times they met. They had said many lively things back then, laughing, crying and sighing, during the first couple times. And

Naimon • 135

then other equally lively things, funny things, deep things, heartbreaking things the third and fourth and even fifth times. The sixth and seventh were certainly good if less lively, less smooth. The eighth and ninth, well, time was doing something to their dance. But for Ismit, he wasn't sure it was time, wasn't sure it mattered to him if they easily had things to say or nothing at all. For Ismit, it was the not telling, the not telling her simply that he wasn't zeroing. Letting the silence, the time speak for him. And Rose not asking. Not even once. It was the time, the accumulated time, of not saying what they both knew.

Rose, as if hearing his thoughts, held her wing over Ismit, like an asymmetrical umbrella, to shade his face from the sun. She took one of his whiskers in her beak and ever so gently pulled his face toward hers. In lieu of kissing they rubbed the sides of their faces together, the soft fur and softer feathers just below and behind each of their eyes in a slow and sweet and quiet caress.

Lots of animals had crazy long and elaborate courtships he knew. And that pigeons were unusually monogamous through it all. But as they searched and listened and searched some more, Ismit looking at his purring cat pressed up against the bird of his life, the bird of his heart, the bird of his future, he wondered if, as the aspiring man, he was supposed to assert the rules. Maybe all this searching and listening was only good for so long. Maybe his original trap and capture, maybe that wasn't so wrong after all. Or maybe it was wrong then but not wrong anymore. Isn't that what cats are supposed to do?

Ismit was confused. The messaging was terribly confused. Each of them getting print-outs of their own animal equivalent deaths. Trying to minimize them, but swimming among them. And yet somehow also here, on screen, loving each other in those same dying bodies. He couldn't wait. He peeked at the top piece of torn paper. Twenty-six calico kitten deaths. The one below: thirty-two calico kitten deaths. The one below that: twenty-nine calico kitten deaths. This wasn't working. This just wasn't working. He put his cat on auto-pilot, took off his Biotarsal, slid out of the kiosk, and leaned over the railing. He turned toward the sound of the central solar refractor as it lifted, rotated and clicked back into place, sending a bevy of crows skyward before they settled again on the refractor's lip. He looked down at all the people half-in and half-out of their thermal suits happily frolicking on the greenway. Laying on the grass, standing on the grass, jumping on the grass. It angered him. He imagined that giant python coming and swallowing them all, one after the next. Then the satiated snake, a giant bolus of humanity bulging its midsection, would unhinge its jaw, and sleep a glorious sleep, a sleep of a day hard earned and well spent, blocking the greenway from anyone but him and his meal. This made Ismit happy. Imagining this. But why was it so complicated? The snake too was on the grass, really crushing the grass.

Walking to Kavic's was a walk of shame. He hadn't been a good friend. Even though his friend had clearly muzzled himself on behalf of their friendship. Ismit had called in a big favor and figured they were now even. Even if Ismit were likely heading back to juvie for skipping Remedial Thought. But he needed Kavic again. Here in the real world. He needed Kavic's help. He needed Kavic's hacking. So he came bearing a gift. The hugest and smelliest Romanian salami he could find. A salami scepter. A saber of a salami. A salami staff suited for the greatest of salami wizards.

Kavic took the meat sword, nodded ceremonially and stood it against the wall behind him as they sat on the floor at his work table. And the smell seemed to work its spell. At least for this brief moment, for this time together, things seemed to be back like they were before.

"So you want me to hack your interface and change your animal?" Kavic said, confused. "That's it? You don't want me to change your score?"

"No not the score." said Ismit. "I can do this Kav. I can zero. I just think the kitty death equivalents are really messing with me. I know it is a disincentivizer and all. But I keep thinking of Rho dying. Like every fifteen minutes." Ismit unclamped the tarsal and handed it across to his friend.

"They give you that toxo plasmo brain invader bug. Cats do," Kavic said. "That mind munching worm that makes you, well, like you are, Iz. A freakin' cat-whisperer."

"That's what I'm saying. I need something else. Something that hasn't put a love bug in me."

"You think you can score without me changing the score?" Kavic smirked.

Ismit couldn't bear the idea of faking his way to Rose. Not by cheating. He just needed to be motivated different. "Just give me something I'd hate. I'll do better if I'm getting read-outs of the deaths of things I hate. If I'm trying to minimize the deaths of things I hate." He flicked a booger at Kavic for emphasis.

"Like flying cockroaches?" Kavic pulled out his species equivalator. "Let's see. You killed three hundred thirty-eight calico kittens this week," he said as he turned the dial. "Good job, man. Now wait a minute, here it is: Six hundred thirty-three thousand two hundred and twenty-one flying cockroaches. You think you're really going to score this way?"

"Reduce my score this way. And there's no way that two thousand cockroaches are worth a calico. No way."

"Right. Reduce your score," Kavic pulled out his arthropod conversion calculator. "What is the thing that would most freak you the fuck out? Maggots? Blowflies? Head lice?" Kavic was getting a kick out of this. "Okay head lice. Ten million two hundred ten thousand five hundred and thirty-eight head lice! You had a great week Iz!"

Sixteen head lice equaled one cockroach. That seemed reasonable to Ismit. But no number of cockroaches could equal a cat. "Head lice it is. Just make sure I'm not going to kiosk with Rose as a louse."

Kavic snorted. "Squirming up into her under feathers."

"Or eating me!"

"Iz, she already has, man. She already has. Just have some love gloves ready. I've got you."

"Yeah," Ismit said, suddenly a little downhearted.

Up until now, Ismit had imagined zero as a worry-free space, a wide open prairie of happiness. When Rose and Ismit found each other there, he'd assumed they'd find freedom there too. Together, wild and wooly, they'd roam. But he'd never owned condoms, didn't know how to put one on, didn't want to fumble or fail in the crucial moment, didn't want to *think* about anything then at all. If he had to, what was the point of all this anyways? *Why was everything so complicated?*

"What did you say?" Kavic responded, Ismit not realizing he was thinking out loud. "Iz, just get the lubed trainers. Then you can freak, like you're gonna do anyways. But at least they'll keep you from being a one pump chump."

"What the hell Kav?" Ismit said. "I say head lice, you say one pump chump? I know what I'm doing, ass-face."

"Just trust me on this. Use the trainers," Kavic said. "The lube, its medicated. It downshifts frontal brain stuff. It'll feel good to Madame Rulemeister too.

"Screw off." Ismit wanted to strangle him, to make his eyes pulse, to rejigger his face until he stopped seeing that Ismit didn't know what he was doing. If Kavic could see it, couldn't Rose too?

He just wanted it to be right, good, nice. Right, good, nice, and *easy*. Or at least easier. Rose had never actually said she didn't think he was trying. But Ismit could feel the words hanging in the air. She'd been waiting on the wide open prairie of happiness for weeks now, alone. That would've made Ismit cranky, too. Even crazy.

While Kavic dismantled the BioTarsal, Ismit remembered that one unforgettable twilight week, post-embedment, pre-separation, when everything was magical. Almost everything. It still hurt him when, in their study vestibule, he went to tickle her through her popliteal vents and she shooed him away. "You my friend are going to flunk Remedial Thought," Rose had said, pointing at his homework. "Think about *that* for a minute." Ismit had shrugged it off. "I hate that class," he said. He tried again beneath the table to make lasting contact but Rose shifted her chair back and resumed reading her book. *How life had changed*, Ismit thought then. Improbably, he had a book now too, Remedial Thought in book form, to better be with Rose. Things had changed so much he hardly recognized himself sitting before a book. He couldn't enter the words, not with the self-consciousness of it all, watching himself read as if he were an actor in a "film." He might as well've had an abacus, shuttling its beads in some hidden code, while clacking his wooden teeth.

But Ismit redoubled his efforts during one of the last times Rose and him had shared a room. He squared himself to the up-lit work surface, rolled his shoulders forward and cradled the book between his outstretched elbows, in a pantomime of Rose. But as he fondled his book the paper bent and creased. The pages squeaked between his fingers or nipped at them like angry insects. And the absurd labor of flipping the pages, over and over again, made thought synthesis impossible for Ismit. Impossible even if Rose were not sitting there across from him, so close, but transported so far away.

Kavic leaned toward Ismit. "Trade secret," he said in a half-whisper, breaking the silence between them. Ismit looked at him and away again.

"*After Yous*," Kavic said.

"Huh?"

"Get the *After Yous*. In the silver box. They're basically the same as the trainers," Kavic said. "Same lube, different packaging. No newbie stigma."

Ismit would never forget what happened next. Not for the rest of his life. "*Fuck*, you suck," he said shoving back from the table. And then, standing up in a wide stance, Ismit grabbed the salami, lifted that Samurai meat sword and swung it with all his might, all his anger, all his confusion and all of his fear, against the side of Kavic's head. He didn't think the salami would deliver its full force. He didn't know that Romanian salami wouldn't break. When Kavic toppled over, grabbed his neck and stormed out of the room, Ismit knew what he had done. When Kavic did this rather than lunging at him with his much larger frame, wrapping Ismit in a death grip bear hug, squeezing the breath out of him while his face mushed like a melon against Kavic's smelly chest, a familiar gamy smell of wet hair, tzatziki and socks worn a week too long, the push-pull smell of friendship, when Kavic didn't do that but did this instead, Ismit knew. The salami didn't break. But something had.

Ismit made one more trip to the kiosk. The eleventh. At first he thought, despite the disaster his life had become, that this was auspicious. One and one, Rose's note had said. Eleven. One minus one. Zero. For the first time, the ache in the hollows on either side of his achilles tendon felt *good*, the polymer TipToe a welcome presence, the pain a longing. But Ismit was in denial. His scores weren't budging. And when he slid into the booth at the kiosk by the sunken greenway and logged himself in, to his dismay, what he saw, displayed there before him, was a grotesque wingless insect, an insect with piercing mouthparts, a biting parasitic insect with a large head and large jaws. He saw himself. A louse. He quickly logged out. And wrote Rose a message:

I need to step back. I need time. To get myself back to my self. —Iz

He hadn't seen her since. He hadn't left his squat, changed his liner, eaten anything but tubes of pea protein paste and ozonated gray water. He wasn't going to see her again until he had something to show for it. Or maybe he was giving up. Yes, that's what he was doing. He was giving up, Ismit thought, as he unzipped his left gaiter vent. He couldn't imagine showing up again with empty hands.

Ismit pressed the outflared lip of the extractor against the bulge in his ankle and closed his eyes. Goodbye Rose, he said, as he waited for the pain. Goodbye, he repeated and bit down on his tongue in anticipation. To fight against self-doubt, he conjured his future, his ground-beef, heated-squat, lolly-gagging on the greenway, messy, outside-the-lines kisses with downsector girls future. But he felt nothing. Nothing at all. Not a pinch, not a pang, not an itch. Nothing.

Fuck my brain, Ismit mumbled. *The flip.* He opened his eyes to find the switch flip, but found Rho glowering a *gimme-me-a-break,-bro* glare at him instead. Rho lifted her osseo-integrative prothesis, the one that nearly bankrupted Ismit to acquire, without releasing Ismit from her gaze. Ismit could swear the cat was trying to communicate with him.

You have to lose something to win? Ismit said on behalf of his cat. *Is that it?*

Of course, Kavic always had razzed Ismit whenever Ismit had insisted that Rho, no ordinary feline, transcended all species categorization. That she was not a cat per se, just a *Rho*.

Ismit did speak with his cat, it's true. But when he "spoke" with Rho, he spoke for both of them. He wasn't crazy. Yet, on the other hand, weren't the words Ismit chose for Rho, that came to him based on how well he knew his furry squat-mate, weren't they coming from Rho in some way, sort of?

Obviously, Rho blinked. Then her eyes— impatient, disdainful, disgusted—deepened in their demand. *Go for broke or go home.*

"Seriously dude?" Ismit said. "You're cool with a veggie-scrapple food downgrade?" Sacrificing Rho's food quality had been a red line before. "No more vole-chickadee nuggets? Huh?" But Ismit needed her onboard now. "And plenty more of that dorky tube sweater you have to wear in here? You onboard with no heat?"

Rho slid off her perch, turned her head away from Ismit, wedged her face straight up her ass, and began a slurp-happy deep clean. But not before firing off one last volley, a *don't be a pussy* scowl that split right through Ismit's self-regard.

Back to kitty death equivalents and fully motivated, Ismit rarely ventured out now. His squat was his laboratory, his alchemical crock pot, his hermetic echo-chamber of ecoimpact mania. Ismit leapt into this experimental playpen with the renewed vigor of a squirrel in springtime. Quickly he learned that if he powered down the lights and relied solely upon algae-lanterns, he could save fifteen kittens. Six more by eating dehydrated bean flakes instead of pea paste. Twenty-five saved from a one day fast, twelve by not swapping out the filter in his thermal suit, a whopping forty-three by not flushing.

But there was a terrible flip side to this. Kittens died in Ismit's sleep, *from* his sleep. Three in fact. They died, or fractions of them did, from every Ismit movement, every Ismit breath. Perhaps every Ismit thought knocked a moment off a kitten's life. It was as if Ismit couldn't *be* without a kitty-death-equivalent.

Confronted with this harrowing kitty calculus Ismit wondered how zero was possible, whether it was something about Ismit himself that caused pain to kittens or to girl-pigeon-platypuses here, there, and everywhere. Maybe there was. Maybe his very existence was a painful thing for the world.

Ismit powered down even the algae-lanterns now, and fogged the south wall's glass apertures to let the descending gloom blur the passage of time and its little deaths. He didn't read the ticker tape anymore. He just tore it off blindly as he puttered around in his squat or let it drag behind him until Rho mangled it apart. He found a book Rose had given him in the good ol' days, one he hadn't bothered to read. One that had propped up the command seat of his now unplugged game console.

Glorious Flight: The Heroic Life and Legacy of Cher Ami. it was entitled. He slid it out from under the seat now and curled up with it beneath the covers of his cot. He opened it to a page dog-eared and feathered by Rose. *War-Time Hero* said the header. It read:

> *In October of 1918, trapped behind enemy lines without food, ammunition, or hope, five hundred Allied soldiers huddled in a small depression against the side of a hill. Woefully exposed, they received fire from both the German troops that surrounded them*

and Allied forces who, tragically, didn't know the location of their trapped compatriots. By the second day, only one-hundred and ninety-four soldiers still drew breath. The situation dire, a homing pigeon was dispatched for help, but it was quickly shot down. Carrying an equally desperate message, a second homing pigeon was dispatched. It too was summarily shot from the sky. Only one homing pigeon now stood between this infantry division and certain death. Cher Ami.

A canister was quickly attached to Cher Ami's left leg, containing a final hangman's hope of a call for help. The lives of these one-hundred ninety-four men rested now on Cher Ami's brave wings. As if on cue, Cher Ami burst forth from the brush, rose through the latticed sky, crisscrossed by the whiz and zip of German bullets, bullets that erred too high or too low as this feathered promise took flight. But Cher Ami, like the brave pigeons that came before, eventually took fire, and dropped from the sky like a stone.

The best of men lose hope down in the dirt. But it is there where heroes are also born. Shot through the breast, covered in blood, blinded in one eye, with a leg hanging by the mere shred of a tendon, Cher Ami somehow took flight once again, flying twenty-five miles to division headquarters in a mere sixty-five minutes, saving all one-hundred ninety-four souls in the process.

Cher Ami received the Croix de Guerre for heroic service, the attention of the best Army medics, a specially carved wooden leg, and a personal farewell from none other than General Pershing himself when Cher Ami's boat departed for America. But it wasn't until Cher Ami passed away, its body being stuffed and mounted for display in the Smithsonian, that it was discovered that Cher Ami, was really Chere Amie, not a he but a she, not a cock but a hen, not a hero but a heroine, that her glorious flight was that of yet another woman unheralded for her courage in this battle of men.

Ismit lifted his head from the book for a moment, disoriented. He dragged his hand delicately across the words he'd just read. He counted the pages he could not remember flipping through, laboriously or otherwise. The very bookness of the book—its heft, its bulk, its pointed angles, the absurd mechanics of its formidable but flimsy interior—had melted away. He had been *with* the bird. He tracked his fingers over a note Rose had written in the margins—*Pigeon Hens Rule!*—and smiled. But the smile fell as quickly as it rose, crashing to earth in a thud of melancholic resignation. Ismit was with the birds, down in the dirt where heroes were born. But he knew he was no Cher Ami.

When the tic-tac-toc of the knocker wakes Ismit, he realizes he has fully succeeded at destroying time. He does not know what day it is, what time of day, whether it is day at all. It's as if life were one perpetual present tense now. Wobbling upright, he steps on the ticker tape. With his toes, he tears off the sleep-accumulated death trailing behind him before shuffling to the ingress.

"Coming," he says, as the tic-tac-toc continues, a brief round of it, then another and another. Kavic likes to torment Ismit this way, he remembers. "Coming," he repeats. But Ismit's legs feel weak and he leans against the sloped wall of the atrium for a moment, overcome with a sudden deep hunger. *When has he last eaten? What has he last eaten?* The knocker persists. "Okay, okay," he mumbles to himself. He rubs his face up and down with his flattened palms to warm it up, to waken his senses, before putting his weight behind the lever.

"What is it?" Ismit says. He lifts his forearm before his eyes, to shield himself against the outside world, the flare of light it produces when he lets it in.

When was the last time he'd seen Kav? Ismit wonders.

"This better be good," he says. "I'm pretty busy grim-reaping in here." Ismit rolls the door open further with his shoulder.

"Iz?" the voice in the light says, thin, disembodied, small. "Oh my god, Iz. You look, you look like a beast."

Rose's hand alights on the wisps of beard that have overtaken Ismit's face. *More like an overgrown garden*, he thinks to say, but she has already pushed past him before he can gather his wits, before his eyes can adjust. Ismit turns slowly and follows her inside, touching the place on his cheek where her hand has just been.

"It looks like wild animals have tore through the place," he hears her say from the back room as he turns. When he gets there, the algae-lanterns have already been reluminesced, the glass apertures defogged. The aerocycle is clattering back to life. But Rose is no longer there. Ismit takes in the room in the muted green glow, seeing it through her eyes—the whirlpool of sheets on the cot, the teetering stack of veggie scrapple tins, the withered tubes of this and that paste. From the bathroom he hears a gasp and then a flush. Several more flushes follow. He nudges the bed pan under his cot and gums a mint-flavored lozenge as he picks sleep from his eyes.

Rose reemerges with Rho, newly sweatered and cradled in her arms. "You two," she says. "You're both so..." Her voice breaks mid-sentence. She pauses as if observing it as it does. She smells Rho between her ears, searching for her next word. "So skinny," she says. "You're both so thin."

Ismit doesn't speak. He can't. He's remembering Rose, seeing her again, seeing her for the first time. She looks more beautiful than ever, brighter, stronger. It pains him.

"I should be mad at you," she says.

"How'd you get here?" Ismit asks. He's never wanted her to see his squat, even in the best of times.

She sets Rho down on the cot and sits on its edge herself. She starts to straighten the sheets, pausing by his pillow, by the open copy of *Glorious Flight* now under her hands. "Did you?" she asks. "Did you really read it? For reals?"

He can't help it. He smiles. Shy, proud, confused, he doesn't want to want.

"Kavic's worried about you," Rose says finally. "He found me. He says it's your birthday."

His birthday? "It's not for a week yet," Ismit says, now uncertain.

"I got you something," Rose says, standing again, fishing in the pockets of her suit. "You ready?" She holds out her hands, one cupped over the other, as she approaches.

They stand close now. Ismit can feel his heart as if every beat is a choice. His lungs ache as if scooped out and hollow. He's conscious of his smell now and wants to step back. Instead he nods.

She opens her hands like a hinged box. Ismit thinks of a coffin, remembers her hand touching his face. Both hands are open now, side by side, curled together into a bowl, a nest. He looks up into Rose's eyes. He searches them, unsure what to feel. Then, he looks again at the powder pink egg nestled in her palms.

"I missed you," she says, an answer to the question he hasn't asked.

Ismit stares at the egg, touches it, takes it from her hands. His ankle twinges. He wonders when she removed it, how. "It's warm," he says.

She leans in and kisses him. Her lips and nose are cold. Her breath tastes fresh, green. He knows how to do this, he reminds himself. But her kiss is different, more open, more imprecise, more unknown than before. He feels lost in it. He wants to be. He anchors himself loosely, his hands on the flared bones of her hips as he follows her lead.

"I missed you too," he says when they come up for air.

Rose removes her hands from his hair and unzips her cuff pocket. She slides out a small silver square. An *After You*.

"I…" she begins.

Ismit shakes his head no, places his hand to her mouth, smiles. He doesn't want to know, though he does sort of suspect it's Kavic's doing. He's touched, embarrassed, scared. *I can't zero*, he wants to tell her. *Something's wrong with me, with the things that I touch.*

But Rose begins to undress him. She opens his vents, starts to roll down his suit, peel off his liner. Goose bumps lift in the cold. He follows her to the cot. It squeaks and teeters when they sit on it, as they slide under the blankets. She's removing her top. He looks at her collarbones, at a red birthmark like a tiny splatter of wine at the top of her left breast. He feels her chest against him, warm and spongy. They begin to move together on their sides, half-clothed.

"How'd you do it?" he whispers, hoping to slow things down. "How'd you zero, Rose?"

"It wasn't that hard," she says into his neck. "I took an advance on my sluice account. There's more than I'll need in there for college."

Ismit shifts up onto an elbow, nods for her to continue. His eyes flit over her naked torso, hers over his.

"You know the exurb greenway they're building?" Rose asks. "I bought some arboreal implants for it. Forty or fifty, I think. That about did it, really," she says. "We should go, it's going to be beautiful there."

"Okay," Ismit says mechanically. "That sounds fun," he says, but he's retreating inward. He can feel it. He waits there, waits to see what it is exactly he's feeling. Sadness, disbelief, grief, a certain absurd hilarity? A little bit of each of these, he thinks. But mostly anger. A different anger than he's felt before, than Kavic-anger. It's reflexive, slow, and gentle; a slow-moving, thick-water stream, a stream spilling over, diverted from its course, a dammed-up stream folded back on itself, fed upon by and feeding his original desire for Rose. It doesn't make sense to Ismit, he can't picture it exactly, he doesn't try to understand it, but the wounding he feels makes his longing stronger, not only because her hands are inside his rain pants, not only because she starts to roll the *After You* down over him, slowly, tenderly with her cool fingers.

He fights himself back now. It's painful to as she touches him there, but once it's on him, he's more than the desire to give himself over. She pushes him back. He's lying backwards. He's traveling at a comfortable pace now, riding that same desire, being ridden by it still.

She moves above him, her hands flat on his chest, her incisors biting down on her lip, her eyes open but out of focus. He's elsewhere too. He thinks of the python, jaws happily unhinged, digesting, daydreaming. He senses a field of wild grasses he can't quite see, just over the ridge. He closes his eyes to search for it but begins to lose his sense of Rose, of himself, when he does.

"Am I hurting you?" she says, slowing down but unable to stop entirely. "You're so quiet," she says, worried.

She speeds up again before he answers, as if the answer isn't the point. He looks down past her hips, past her naked calves and ankles to either side of his thighs. He smiles as Rho's prosthetic paw swipes at the tape sputtering from his Biotarsal, cascading over the end of the cot as they move.

"Yes," he answers, closing his eyes. "Yes, Rose, yes."

*Female flagger, Oregon State Highway Dept., circa WWII.
Oregon Department of Transportation.*

Sayantani Dasgupta in conversation with Tara Roberts
Spring 2022

Sayantani Dasgupta was born in Calcutta, India and raised in New Delhi. She arrived in Moscow, Idaho in 2006 to enroll in an MFA program at the University of Idaho and ended up living there for twelve years. Today, she is an assistant professor of creative writing at the University of North Carolina Wilmington, where she writes both fiction and nonfiction. She is the author, most recently, of a short story collection, *Women Who Misbehave*, which was published in 2021.

Tara Roberts is a freelance writer and part-time lecturer in the University of Idaho English Department, as well as the editor of *Project FARE*, a nonprofit digital magazine about food in Idaho.

Roberts

I want to start with one of my favorite moments in the book, in "Miss Josephine," when the narrator remembers how she and her friends suppressed their greed for ice cream as young teenagers but kept going to the ice cream shop out of lust for the boys who hung out there. What are your favorite sins to write about—and what are your favorite sins to commit?

Dasgupta

I think lust definitely is a great sin to think about, because I feel most women are not given the agency to do that. And I don't think it's mostly Indian women or women of a certain age, but women overall, all over the world. I think lust is something most of us are encouraged to hold back and conform, and I don't think men have similar limitations imposed, as far as their imagining of the sin is concerned.

From a writing point of view, I think lust is great fun to imagine, because what everyone's lusting for is different, and who gets to be their object of affection is different. When I'm writing fiction, to be able to inhabit these different characters and their different worlds, and think about what someone like this would be attracted to is, I think, a great mental exercise and a huge challenge. I'm not these people, but I have to think like different people and what they could find attractive in other people. It's a little bit like in real life, when you sometimes see couples and you kind of wonder what brought them together. Because on the surface, you can't see it, you can't see the attraction, but maybe there's something else to them. It forms such an interesting challenge in my mind.

My favorite to commit? Oh, I think gluttony. Why is it so *good?* I was in India for a little while this winter, and most of me was so happy with all the food choices there. But a small part of me was also missing all the American foods I have come to love! So I think my happy place would be somewhere in the middle of the world where I just have access to all the gluttonous goodness everywhere.

Roberts

Me too—so let's talk about food in your book. It's absolutely everywhere. I made a list: lamb biryani, spaghetti and meatballs, puffed rice snacks, apple strudel, canned tuna, and then your last story is all about hunger. What makes food such a powerful and malleable image to work with?

Dasgupta

Food is such a telling statement of who you are as a person. I think you can fake a lot of things in life. You can pretend to be sophisticated or not through a variety of lenses. But what food you love is a very good revelation of who you are as a person. You can't pretend to love things to eat and commit yourself to that. Or maybe you can but that will just not be a very happy life. I think food is also interesting because, again, it's a challenge imagining what different people in different circumstances would be attracted to. If I'm not these people, but I want them to be convincing, then I want to know what they eat for breakfast, what they eat for lunch, dinner. What are their guilty pleasures in terms of treats, what is their favorite cake, those sorts of things.

One time Kim Barnes had us think in these lines in class, because she said if you're writing fiction, you have to know about the toilet paper brand that your character uses. That is the level of detail you must know. It doesn't matter if there is no mention of toilet paper in the story. But the more you know, the more your reader will know that you know. Even when I'm not necessarily incorporating everything that a character loves to eat, I definitely imagine what all they love to eat so that I get a fuller picture. And of course there are people who don't care about food that much—I don't understand such people, but I'm told that they exist. So I think I'm just going to remain suspicious of them because they don't fit into my orbit and understanding of what good characters in fiction should be.

Roberts

I have to ask the big misbehavior question, which I feel like is a given, but an important one. We see a dramatic range of so-called misbehavior throughout the book—from little things like breaking cultural norms to selfishness to some very big crimes that I don't want to reveal. How do you define what it means for a woman to misbehave?

Dasgupta

Growing up, the world of women that I saw on television, in real life, in books, in my neighborhood, school, everywhere, it seemed that there were so many secret messages. There were things that were not being said out loud, but they were implied; they were to be understood. There was a lot of reading you had to do based on your equation with the person. And I think that was true when I came to the U.S. as well. I felt women have to live here, too, by their own code. You can't say everything that comes to your mind. You can't do everything that comes to your mind.

One of the things that was most surprising to me when I first came to the U of I was how few women were in upper administration. If you don't grow up in America, the narrative of America that you receive is it is this progressive, egalitarian land where everyone gets the same opportunities. And yet I remember going up to a room where all the university presidents' pictures are kept, and there is only one lady in that entire area of gray-haired white gentleman. The whiteness was not difficult to understand, given it's northern Idaho, but the lack of anybody except one female president was kind of shocking. The university has been around for a while, so it just didn't make sense for that to be the case.

I think anyone who, in any which way, even the minutest way, protests against what is expected of her is misbehaving. I'm so drawn to that behavior, and I'm here to champion that behavior, especially selfishness. I think my entire book is a tribute to selfishness. Selfishness is a lovely thing. I think—no, I know—when I was growing up, the model of femininity that was shown to me over and over again, on television particularly, was one where the women who were sacrificing for their brothers, for their fathers, for their husbands were like goddesses. These were the best women. I saw that behavior in women in my life. And I think you miss out on a lot if you are not selfish, because if you don't take care of yourself first and foremost, that's terrible. You are not able to give to others what they probably need and want because you have not served yourself the way you need to. So I'm here to say that selfishness is beautiful and everyone should embrace it.

Roberts

You also write about women who say they want to be a good girl or a good woman. What does it mean to be good?

Dasgupta

Particularly in the story "Shaaji and Satnam," there is a moment where Shaaji, even when she's committing something deeply problematic, she's thinking of how she can be a good girl. I've seen a lot of people, including myself, who have been raised with a fair amount of discipline, and what it means to be on your good behavior, etc., that before committing anything, we're in our heads thinking, "What will my dad say if he finds out?" I think that's what, to an extent, it means to be good—it's the conditioning in your head, that's been done by your teachers, by your family, by yourself, the policing that you've done on yourself, and you're constantly measuring whether that is good behavior.

Roberts

I love that even though we grew up in such wildly different places, we had, I think, similar expectations of policing our own behavior as children that that just hang on. So what do we do about that? How do we deal with enculturated expectations of goodness?

Dasgupta

I know how to deal with that. We read a lot. We read books by people who don't look or sound like us. In my case, the first clear message that I can do something else than what perhaps a lot of girls my age wanted to do was when I read *Twenty-Thousand Leagues Under the Sea*. Captain Nemo, who is a prince of Indian origin, was going to just kidnap people in his submarine and take them off to Antarctica and explore the world. That was *amazing*. I wanted nothing more than Captain Nemo. And the fact that in the book he's described in such a hot way made it even hotter.

You read books that are unexpected, that have nothing to do with your reality. I think you read a lot of sci-fi and fantasy and all kinds of wild fiction that gives you all kinds of permission that realistic fiction and creative nonfiction don't. You imagine yourself doing epic things as a kid. And all those things stay with you. I'm all for reading all the wild literature that's possible in the world.

Roberts

Now I want to talk about secrets. I'm thinking in particular of in "A Hard Kind of Love," where we follow this man who's married to a writer who mines conflict in their marriage for her stories. This is kind of a common question to ask writers, but a lot of times we treat it like it's universal and it's really not—it's something everyone decides individually. So for you, is anything sacred or private? How do you teach your students to navigate that?

Dasgupta

Yes, a lot of things are definitely sacred and private. I might write about them, but I might not publish them. Oftentimes, when I'm angry at someone, I will compose a detailed email to that person. I'll never send it. But having written that out, it helps in sort of calming me down, seeing things in that conflict that were probably my fault as well. A lot of things within the family are sacred and private, and I'm not there yet where I can write about them publicly—which is not to say I'm not writing about them privately. I think all of us should be writing about these things privately.

With students, I encourage them to write their entire truths in the first drafts that they don't have to share with anyone. But I think there is much to be said, from a writerly point of view, about the benefit of our first draft being *everything* that you can think of on that subject. And let that be a 50-page draft for a two-page essay if need be. Once it's out, you still have full control of your material. And you can choose what you want to share with the world.

So I'm a big fan of multiple drafts, and multiple private drafts if need be before the public one is shared. Big fan of students reading a variety of work by incredibly courageous writers like Cheryl Strayed and Kim Barnes. And knowing that once you tell your story authentically, people might still judge you, but they have no control over you. They can't do anything to ruin you. You own your story. Putting out honest writing is a bit like being a straightforward, honest person in the world. Some people will like you, some people won't like you, and that is their effing problem. You get to be yourself.

Roberts

Because *Moss* is a journal about the Pacific Northwest, I have to ask a Pacific Northwest question. Your book shows us a little bit of the Northwest: from the inside in "The Waitress," in a tacky bar full of dark secrets, and from the outside in "Another Life," with the postcards the narrator gets from her brother. How else does the Pacific Northwest sneak into this book?

Dasgupta

I didn't think the Pacific Northwest was a huge part of the book until I moved to the South. But of course it was. I realized this when I finished the book and submitted it to my editor. The Pacific Northwest was a part of the book the whole time I lived in Moscow, because how can you write about anything in your life without taking in the background and the surroundings in which you find yourself? The Northwest also featured heavily in my first book, *Fire Girl*, because *Fire Girl* is a book about making sense of this in-between life between India and America. I think if instead of Moscow, I had lived somewhere like Seattle or San Francisco, where there are so many Indians, my understanding of myself would have been different. But because I landed in Moscow, Idaho, with maybe 10 more Indians in the town on a good day, it made me understand myself in a in a more fundamental way than I think I could have been allowed anywhere else, and get a sense of the kinds of people I value and the kinds I don't want in my life. That understanding has also been cemented over time because of living in places like Idaho, where I am one of very few people who look like me.

In the South, I go back to the Northwest because I lived in the Northwest twelve years, and I have tons of friends and good memories and lots of good people in my life, and I carry all that memory, all that goodness, in my heart. Which is not to say that the Northwest is an uncomplicated place. It's also not to say that liberal pockets like Seattle, even parts of Moscow, parts of Idaho, don't have their own prejudices, don't have their own racism. All of these things definitely filter into everything I write.

Roberts

I want to wind down with a fun question—my students right now are writing an essay about a song, and I've been talking to them about the metaphorical backpack that everyone carries around, with books and movies and products and TV shows and fads and all these things that make their way into our writing and our personalities. What's in your backpack—what are the things that shape you as a writer? What do you wish more Americans would engage with?

Dasgupta

I really want Americans to start looking at maps and atlases and globes. I absolutely want people to stop saying things like, "I didn't know there were more than 10 languages in the world." Or "I cannot point to Canada on a map." These are both things I have had people say to me. I do not want ever for anyone to ask me if India is a real country.

But I think overall for humanity, I would just like people to be more curious. I think that would be lovely. You can just give into any kind of curiosity. Why is that bird flying in that odd way? What is something around your own world that is of interest to you or piques your curiosity?

In my own backpack: Hindi films, for sure. Indian music—and I make the distinction between Hindi films and Indian music because India has many languages and many cultures, and Hindi is just one language. Folktales, fairy tales, Hindu mythological tales that I grew up reading as a kid. Books by British authors that I grew up reading as a kid. I love Agatha Christie, Enid Blyton, all sorts of adventure novels, like *Twenty-Thousand Leagues Under the Sea*, which I've already mentioned, and *The Swiss Family Robinson*, which is so wonderful. I remember reading that one and telling my dad, "What are the chances of us landing on an island and then rebuilding our lives?" And my dad, who was an engineer in a big city, must have been like, "Oh God, I do not want to live in an abandoned island and have to figure out how to farm." That family's protecting themselves from giant pythons, and there is a pet ostrich—everything that can happen happens to that family, and that was so amazing, but I don't think my dad was particularly keen on that being our future life.

Food, of course. I need some spicy food. I can probably do three days of standard American food, maybe. But the fourth day, if there is nothing with lots of peppers and spices in my diet, I'm just going to cry. I say three days because based on residencies and such things, where they have provided food, for the first three days I'm like, "Oh my gosh, I don't have to cook!" but then by the fourth day my inner voice says, "Oh my gosh, I want to cook."

I think colors, fragrances, these sorts of things. When I first came to the U.S., I thought America did not have a distinct smell. I thought Moscow particularly did not have a smell. Because Delhi has smells—food smells, people smells, all kinds of things—and Moscow felt very antiseptic and very clean. And it seemed that, what would this world know of anything that's painful or problematic, because everyone is so shiny and gleaming and the houses are perfect and the backyards are perfect and everybody for some strange reason eats dinner at five. I think now after having lived here for so long, I maybe understand that a little bit.

Door Stoop
CMarie Fuhrman

I remember her left hand on the handle holding open the screen door of my childhood home. I see how thin her skin has become, how the light pink she painted on her nails has chipped. Her right hand is open as if waiting for a gift or a grasp. I am standing outside. I have just accused my mother of not loving me.

Behind my mother, my father sits at our kitchen table, but I cannot see him. I know she has placed food in front of him, and that he is merely staring at it. He will push the plate away and call for her. He will say, *where are you?* as if she is the only *you*. She will hesitate, her hand still on the door that came with the house they bought in '66. The gray duct tape will hold the tear in the screen. The door will slam when the glass is pushed up, and it will catch the wind when the glass is closed. My mother will remind us of this every time we pass through.

The handle is grey like the sky between storms. There is a ridge running down the center, either side of the ridge is smooth, but the crest of that line is sharp. This my child thumb would have avoided.

My father is in the seventh year of Alzheimer's and will die in six months. I have returned home to help my mother. When finally I returned home and walked through the front door, my father pointed at me, "You," he said, "get out." Mom asked if he remembered me, "That's Cindy. Our daughter." Again, he unholstered his finger, repeated the words. So I rented a room in town with a yard for my dogs and a window too high to stare out of. I spent my days shopping, evenings on long runs. I slept with men who had my father's education and his new disregard. It felt like something I could do. A ridge to run my thumb down.

My mother was my father's sole caregiver. I had come home because of 2 a.m. phone calls, her voice breaking 680 miles south. She would be sitting at the kitchen table. Medication and unopened bills next to Oreo cookies--the only food my father would eat. She told me she had to lock the door. She had to put a chain around the gate. *I need you*, she cried.

The door stoop I'm standing on is new. The one of my early childhood was narrow, would never allow this conversation. Four O' Clocks would have covered the trellis, raucous blossoms spiting Northern Colorado sun. The concrete beneath me would be bare of footprints. Only when my father replaced the stoop did he smooth the mud and ask my sister and me to place our right feet in the cement, dip in our initials and the date, 1980. My sister went first.

When it was my turn to step in the cement, my father had said, "Walk softly, Bug." He held both my hands. I barely touched my toes to the wet, felt the cool move up my leg. When it was done, he sat me on the lawn, washed my feet with cold water from a thick green hose, his big fingers tickling one sole, then the other. I fell back in the grass laughing. The sky was a faultless blue.

I have often wondered how I will know who I am after my mother dies. When my sister and I clean out the house. Sell the silverware, the dishes, the kitchen chairs. When her clothes have been cleared from closets, Skin-so-Soft poured down the drain. After the phone is disconnected and the house sells and new owners rip up the carpet, replace locks, paint the house a lighter shade of yellow, or worse. Will I drive by that house on Lela Lane, stare past the empty passenger seat through the window to a door stoop where two ghosts stand. Will I recognize the little girl whose name is forever on the step, or the grown woman whose words were a blade I drew and wielded at my mother. Will I afford the emptiness that is mine the same love I demanded of my mother the summer afternoon?

My mother's lips are always painted. So careful to look nice. Even then. Exhausted, the sleeves of her blouse pushed up to her elbows, bruised skin from my father's demented grip. My mother's eyes are green. Her name is Dolores, which means sorrow, and the words that I said to her, the words cut into the transom above a door I could not go through, found her ears, fell to her stomach, took so much of her breath that she could say only three words back to the sentence I spoke because the men and the gym, the miles run, and money spent were not enough to dull the pain of my father's dying and my need to be her little girl, the one who wanted so badly to come in and be eight again, feet wet, my father's big arms holding me while Mom wrapped me in a towel. She would put her left hand against my dumb cheek and repeat the words I needed to hear. As if it didn't show. As if I were the only *you* and she could love only me.

Islands FIA Crew.
USDA Forest Service, Pacific Northwest Research Station, 2016.

Futures
Ayana Harscoet

introduction

    post-Superfund designation, it begins with maybe. maybe we will find it. maybe it will be hidden in the metrics. maybe we will find it at the intersection of 1st Ave S and E. Marginal Way or at the crossroads of hydrologic planning and bioengineering. maybe it's a hypothesis and maybe it isn't. maybe it defies what is. whatever may be, it begins somewhere near the opening at elliott bay and trickles upstream with the rising tide.
    there are a number of research questions. here is the question: is it possible? here is a question: what deepens? here for good measure is another question: what spills over? here is a measurement for good practice: 1,400 ppm. here is a methods section and here is an overflow and here is an emptiness waiting to be new.

just think—
with the right tools
and strategic techniques

we[1] are right on the verge
of almost knowing.

methods

flatten the intertidal at Herring's House
(store in GIS/ArcView software)

                      crack the armored shoreline

get intimate with the data:
identify restoration sites:

- relict patches embedded
- in an industrialized landscape
- undoubtedly compromised

1. U.S. Fish and Wildlife Service
School of Aquatic & Fishery Sciences, University of Washington
School of Marine and Environmental Affairs, University of Washington

fix samples in 5% buffered formaldehyde   transfer to 50% isopropanol

develop criteria
      (best to have at least nine
      physical and biological)

don't forget to ask salmon
to diagnose the ecological state

or shake coarse sand
through nested sieves
(#10, #18, #35, #60, #120, #130)
if necessary, forgo placekeeping
for pacemaking. fixate
on return, or settle
for approximation.

arrive with toolbox overflowing
with protocols and procedures and methods sections and plunge gloved hands into the current.

become a publication, a citation,
a cover page, a precedent.

renew the search.

results

what lies at the end
or something like that

discussion

will be known in due time.

Notes

Much of the first page of the methods section in this poem is found language, drawn from the following scientific reports and papers: *Elliott Bay/Duwamish Restoration Program: Year 1 Intertidal Habitat Projects Monitoring Report*; *Ecological Effects of Shoreline Armoring on Intertidal Habitats of a Puget Sound Urban Estuary*; *Biological Monitoring at Duwamish River Coastal America Restoration and Reference Sites: A Seven-Year Retrospective*; *Duwamish River Coastal America Restoration and Reference Sites: Results from 1995 Monitoring Studies*; and *Elliott Bay/Duwamish Restoration Program: Duwamish/Diagonal CSO/SD Cleanup Study Report*.

La Forestal

Rita Sturam Wirkala

> *Everything lasted as long as the blood lasted,*
> *the back, the heart, the arm hacking*
> *in the red hell of the quebracho.*
> —Rafael Lelpi

Foreword

I received the sad news of my mother's death while I was in East Timor, in the midst of the celebrations—and chaos—over Indonesian independence. I had to fly from one hemisphere to the other and was late for the funeral in Argentina, but I applied myself to selecting some of her belongings for myself and deciding what to do with others. In the process, I came across a journal from my youth. I leafed through it eagerly finding a lot of nonsense and a single treasure: my account of an event that I had certainly never forgotten, although the details had become fuzzy. I had typed it on my old Olivetti (I was always aware of my sloppy handwriting) and folded and glued the sheets to a notebook. I kept it for another two decades and have recently taken to transcribing it.

Although I have had to edit the language, the narrative is true to the events that occurred over two turbulent days in Tartagal during that leap year of 1972.

Friday

The mayor's young wife met me at the bus station. Her husband was away traveling but she would take me to speak with the president of the cultural committee, who was aware of my visit.

Her name was Lucía. When I asked her to direct me to a hotel, she responded, "I won't hear of it, you're staying with us!" I didn't wait for her to ask again. Since hers was the home of a town official, there would surely be hot water.

"Felicia, take the lady's suitcase!" she said. Only then did I notice a girl who had been keeping her distance. She was slim, with golden-brown skin, and she gazed at me through long, dark bangs.

"No, I'm fine. It's light," I said.

"I won't hear of it!" Lucía protested.

I had no choice but to accept her forceful offer.

On the way to their house, I made out a tall, reddish tower in the distance that seemed to be built of brick.

"What's that?" I asked Lucía.

"What?"

"The tower."

"Oh, it's a chimney. It's no longer in use."

I realized later that, although the tall smokestack towered over the flat terrain could be seen from any point or angle, it had blended with the urban landscape, and the inhabitants had stopped seeing it—much like people no longer notice light poles. With a little imagination, we could have been gazing at a minaret in the Middle East. Or standing in front of the Torre Rossa in Italy.

We walked about five blocks and arrived at the house—it was not at all impressive, but it had an ornate garden.

As soon as we went in, they offered me a *mate*.

"Thank you, Lucía. I can't—it's hard on my liver." Certainly, mate is one of my country's few gaucho customs that I have never acquired.

"Oh, then I'll make you some mint tea."

That wasn't a favorite of mine either—my body was clamoring for coffee—but I politely accepted it. Then Felicia appeared with a tray of sugary quince cupcakes that tasted like grandmothers and childhood. Those I devoured.

Lucía asked me many questions about my family, if I had a boyfriend, if I'd ever had one, if I wanted to get married. I didn't want to tell her that for years an assortment of unlikely characters had paraded through my life; that I had changed boyfriends as often as I changed rented rooms, and that none of these transitory loves—much like those impersonal lodgings—felt like "mine." I wanted an intelligent man, someone intellectually curious, sensitive, maybe a poet... Apparently, I only attracted idiots. I made up some stories for her. My world was as distant from Lucía's as my musical career was from Hollywood's tinsel town.

To change the subject, I told her about my "mission" in Tartagal. I explained the town was the beneficiary of a national program for cultural development in the Chaco area, and the orchestra from the neighboring province of Corrientes, where I worked as an oboist, had sent me as its first emissary.

"Tomorrow I'm taking you to meet the chair of the committee," Lucía said, happy to have a role in the project. "Would you like to take a bath?" she asked.

"I would love to!" I replied. I needed a hot bath but didn't know what to expect. I was still wary of the heating device, with its grim electric cables exposed, at my boarding house in Corrientes. I had once heard of someone being electrocuted while taking a shower.

"Felicia, prepare the bath for the señorita."

Carrying a metal cruet, the girl walked me to the bathroom She poured the bottle's contents into a circular receptacle that was located under the small water tank above the showerhead. Then she turned on the faucet, lit a cotton swab with a match, inserted it into the vessel, and *boom!* A circle of fire surrounded the tank. I drew back.

"Ready, Miss. The water will be hot in no time. Do you need me to scrub your back?"

"No, no, Felicia, I'm fine. Thank you," I said and closed the door, thinking of Brunhilda and the magic circle of fire of the Nibelungen in Wagner's opera.

In the end, what I surmised was an alcohol heater, turned out to be more manageable than the hideous electric one with its ominous wires. By the time the fuel had burned off and the flames were out, I was rid of the grime from my long journey.

Since there were no men in the house, I didn't mind leaving the bathroom wrapped in a towel.

"I put your suitcase in Doña Lucía's bedroom," Felicia announced. It hadn't occurred to me to ask where my room was, but now it became obvious there wasn't a guestroom, and I was going to share sleeping quarters with Lucía. Only when I entered the room did I notice there was just one bed: a double one.

I got dressed, plucked up my courage and went to the kitchen to ask, "Lucía, where will I sleep? On the couch in the living room?"

"I won't hear of it! I already told you my husband is traveling, so we can both sleep in the big bed."

I just nodded, speechless. No, I wasn't dreaming. It seemed I would sleep next to my hostess, who I had only just met. I knew there was nothing suspicious in her proposal; it was just her naïve, country way of being hospitable.

Then Lucía noticed my shoes, the same ones I'd been wearing when I got off the bus.

"Felicia! Clean Miss Rita's shoes!"

"That's not necessary, Lucía. I'll wipe them with a rag right now."

"I won't hear of it!"

I couldn't refuse. I was about to take off my footwear when Felicia appeared with a box, the kind shoeshine boys use, and gestured for me to put my right foot up. My heart froze. Here was a girl my age, kneeling on the floor with her body bent towards me, cleaning my shoes! A visceral rejection filled my mouth with protests, but I held them back.

I wanted to close the distance between us and show that I saw her as more than a trained pet, so I asked her some questions while she polished my shoes.

At one point she turned to Lucía and said a few words that were incomprehensible to me, which sounded like *Pu'ama pituma ... karú?* Her employer replied, *Heé ... Ko aga ...* I knew they were speaking Guaraní because I had heard it spoken in Corrientes, and I surmised that Felicia came from that province.

"Lucía, where did you learn Guaraní?"

"From my babysitter when I was little."

Suddenly I was envious of my hostess, who seemed so simple, so convinced of her rights as a white woman in her little fiefdom, so comfortable in her class and so boxed in what I so as her intellectual misery, one that she could not see and yet, she was bilingual! And I, the more educated, a university graduate, only knew my maternal Spanish and a handful of Italian words from the musical lexicon: *Fortissimo... Allegro ma non troppo ... Cantabile*. And others like that.

Perhaps to show off her language skills, Lucía continued to order Felicia around in the maid's indigenous language. To my ears it sounded like a cascade of sweet notes pressed from a cluster of intoxicating fruit, reverberating, intimate and ancient, with an occasional swallowing of vowels and a jungle accent on the final syllable of the high-pitched words. But it was beyond my understanding, from beginning to end.

Once finished with her task, Felicia went to the kitchen. With one quick gesture, she gathered up her thick, straight, dark hair—which fell like a heavy cloak down her back—and secured it with a rounded comb. Then she then put on a cap and a white apron. I looked at my shoes: they shone like two black beetles.

We ate locro for dinner, a northern dish of white corn, pork and onion, and drank wine. Felicia served us in the dining room; she ate in the kitchen after she had cleared the table. I was not surprised.

I-won't-hear-of it! and I went out to walk off our dinner, no small feat after the meal we just had. She told me about a women's charity group she belonged to. And then, too early for my liking, we went to bed.

There was no reading that night, or much conversation. After quickly reciting the *Lord's Prayer* for us both, my bedmate switched off the light, said good night, turned over, and fell asleep. She slept like a baby, within the peace of her well-defined universe, where everything is as it is, and with the sweet certainty that, as it is and was, it would always be. At least that was my perception. My mind, on the other hand, navigated a sea of uncertainties while my bones tried to adjust themselves to the wool mattress.

I remembered then that my grandfather had taught us a game in which each playing card represented a traveler gathering with others at an inn—soldier, nun, merchant, harlequin, blacksmith, and so on. Beds were in limited supply and had to sleep two people each, and bedmates were chosen by dealing cards. (f the soldier's card was dealt on top of the nun's, or vice versa, my grandfather laughed joyfully and uttered comments in his Italian dialect that he never translated for us.) I always thought that this game, fun as it was, did not really reflect human behavior. The game was playfully absurd. But later I learned from some nineteenth-century novels that, not long ago, the definition of privacy was more elastic. People of the same sex didn't mind sharing a bed when necessary, just as today we don't mind sharing a table with a stranger in a crowded cafeteria. What was unusual was that the custom had survived, up to the end of the twentieth century, in the sophisticated homeland of Borges and Cortazar. I had to rethink my assumptions. People who trust one another sleep together, I concluded, and I should feel honored.

But of course, Lucía and I were cut from the same cloth.

Saturday

A commotion of birds I could not identify entered my dream, shrieking like an out-of-tune violin, and waking me up before my hostess at seven in the morning.

I asked the Guaraní girl, who was already busy in the kitchen, if there was coffee in the house. She climbed onto a bench and found a jar of Nescafe that had gone stone hard with age. It tasted awful, but the caffein was manna from heaven.

The window was open, and the air felt strange and heavy. The birds were restless. While Felicia prepared fried cakes, I ventured to ask her about her life.

"Where are you from, Felicia?"

"From over there in the woods, as if you were going to Villa Ana."

"But your family is from Corrientes, right? You speak Guaraní."

"Yes, Miss. My parents came from there."

"Did you go to school?"

"I made it to third grade." She lowered her head.

"What does your dad do?"

"He died," she said, crossing herself.

"I'm sorry… How did he die, do you know?"

"They say he got a lot of sawdust in his lungs."

"Sawdust? From what?"

"He worked at the sawmill."

"Oh, I see. Are there many of those around here?"

"There were, but not anymore. The company closed a few years ago."

"What company was that?"

"La Forestal. Have you never heard of it?" Felicia looked at me as though I had come from Mars.

La Forestal. It sounded vaguely familiar. I asked her to tell me about it. She explained her uncle had been one of the first workers in the English gringos' factories that squeezed the tannin from the red quebracho. Noticing my inquisitive expression, she added, "If you want, I'll take you home so you can talk to my uncle. He knows the whole story. Today is Saturday. It's my day off until mid-afternoon."

Her tone was humble, but I detected a hint of determination in her voice. Or her look.

"But please don't tell Señora Lucía, because she's against..." she added, lowering her voice.

"Against what?"

"What people in the woods say about La Forestal."

A short while later Lucía appeared in the kitchen and invited me to a meeting of the *Acción Católica*. I made up an excuse and then saw she was somewhat disappointed. She had been going to introduce me to some ladies in the charity group.

"Maybe this afternoon?" I suggested. The question hung in the air. Then she said that she would try to arrange something for later if it didn't start raining.

I remembered then that this was the time of year when the Santa Rosa storms broke out in these parts, a few days before or after the celebration of the Latin America's patron saint.

After Lucía left, Felicia made a couple of sandwiches and wrapped them in a kitchen towel, which she put in her sisal twine bag. Outside, brown clouds were gathering on the horizon.

We walked for ten minutes before leaving the town behind and following a trail that soon narrowed between bushes that overran the path. Felicia was in front, walking fast and pushing the foliage aside with both arms, and moving with a grace that would have been the envy of a willow tree, had there been one.

—<o>—

In half an hour we reached the house. It was an adobe hut, with a clay oven in the courtyard, a brick cistern, and a windmill. Under the sparse shade of a budding carob tree, a man sat on the leather seat of a three-legged folding stool. He was sharpening the tip of a stick with a knife. Felicia introduced us and then brought me another triangular stool.

Questions swirled in my brain, stumbling one after another, wanting to get out. I reined them in while Felicia served carob tea, which I gladly accepted.

Don Ramiro and I spoke for a long time in a somewhat disorganized way, but basically his story was this: In his father's time, the Argentinian government had sold the whole expanse where red quebracho grew, an immense territory that encompassed three provinces, to the British.

"And did they buy Tartagal as well?" I asked.

"Tartagal didn't exist, Miss," Felicia's uncle replied. "The foreigners founded it. They founded Tartagal, La Guillermina, Villa Ana, La Galletera ... And those are just the ones remaining today. There were a bunch of towns, more than forty in all, each with its own factory. The British built houses, opened roads, constructed ports on the Paraná River to take away the logs, planks, and tannin to Europe. They also laid four hundred seventy kilometers of railroad track. It was a country within a country, you understand. With its own printed money, police, judges, and everything else."

"Did they have that much capital?"

"Sure. And they made more money during World War One, because the tannin they extracted from the quebracho was used to dye the soldiers' leather boots and belts, the saddles, and who knows what else. Have you seen the factory yet?

"No."

"It was called Quebracho Argentina. And well, only the ruined machines and the chimney are left. The Tobas Indians lived here. The government took their land from them and sold it to the British, and the new owners used Tobas laborers to chop down the trees."

"Their own trees!"

"Yes, their own stolen trees. The wood was also used to make ties for the railroad tracks I mentioned, because quebracho is a fine, fine wood. And extremely hard!"

Colonialism—and the racism it brings with it—here we go again, I thought.

"But those poor Tobas weren't enough for them," Don Ramiro continued. "They went looking for labor in Corrientes. That's how father came to be here. He was promised the sun and the moon, but later he changed his mind and hung out with the strikers. I was little, but I remember. The thing is, people worked twelve hours a day, and were paid a pittance, not with Argentine money but with money those people printed themselves. You could only exchange that so-called currency for food in the company stores—one bill for sugar, another for a little bit of yerba mate, and so on. Even that wasn't enough. At the end of the month, either we filled our bellies with mate, just bitter, or we ended up in debt to the grocery store they owned. There were health problems and many accidents. That's why the workers organized themselves, went on strike, and ended in a massacre."

"A massacre?"

"Yes. Their answer was 'bullets and more bullets.' They killed six hundred workers."

"Six hundred! Oh my God! Was it their thugs, their private police, that did this?"

"The company had its own private police force, true, armed with Mauser rifles, but this time they requested reinforcements from Buenos Aires, and from there they sent a group called, if memory serves, the 'Argentine Patriotic League.' They were paid police, mercenaries, as they say."

Paramilitaries, I muttered. I was familiar with the slogan *patriotic*; the kind of jargon far-right reactionaries now lay claim to.

"Those who were caught alive were tortured so they would give up names and implicate others. And those who escaped were chased through the forest and hunted down like birds, like animals. The union leader was dispatched, poor guy ... they gunned him down in this town's main street. And in the end the prisoners were transported by wagon to the capital. They said they were anarchists. It was an open wagon with many stakes to which they bound the accused, who were forced to stand, all the way to Buenos Aires. And take note, Miss—all this approved by the provincial government!"

"Do you know what happened to those prisoners?"

"Nobody knows. Either they rotted in jail, or they were tortured and killed."

Why don't we know about these events? I asked myself. At school we were taught about the two English invasions of the nineteenth century. But this one? This other piece of British empire established in this country? Or were the hurt and shame too recent?

"So, after that massacre, I suppose there were no more union movements," I added.

"Who would have dared! They started watching us very closely, right up to the day they packed their things and left." Don Ramiro sipped his tea and then turned to the door. "Isidoro, come here and explain to this young lady about *La Forestal*."

The boy who appeared was slender and taller than the hut's doorframe, and his gaze was intense. He greeted me shyly and sat down next to Don Ramiro under the carob tree. It was already midmorning by then, and the crisscrossing shadows of the branches formed a latticework over their faces. It made me think of a moving jail with bars that shifted but allowed no one to exit.

Whatever he knew, he had heard from his father, Isidoro told me, because he was only ten years old when the company left Argentina, a year too young to work hacking down trees. He did remember the number of people who were unemployed from one day to the next.

"They loaded their things and their children onto their carts and went to the cities to look for work," he said.

"But why did the factory close?"

"Why? Because they ran out of trees! They cut down everything in the three provinces. Quebracho takes a hundred years to grow, and no Christian, no Englishman even, can last a hundred years... So they went off to look for other similar trees and found the mimosa, as they call it, in Africa. But before leaving they dismantled all the towns they had built, except for a few of them, like this one, Tartagal."

"If the gringos no longer occupied the land, why didn't the unemployed people stay here and use the soil to grow crops like corn, for example, as they do in the south of the province?" I asked.

The old man picked up a clump of dirt and crumbled it in his hands, sprinkling the ground with dry earth.

"Crops? Nothing grows here, my friend. Look at this poor soil, as cracked as my own face. A graveyard of stumps was all that was left on the useless land."

"The thing is, when there are no trees or grass, the rainwater wipes out all the good layers of soil," Isidoro explained.

I thought about the delicate balance of life. And I began to understand how in recent years the population of the so-called shantytowns had grown so fast on the outskirts of the cities. We knew they came from north of Santa Fé, from the Chaco, from Santiago del Estero, but not why. We were unaware of the overwhelming reality along the so-called 'tannin route.' What's more, deforestation was not a word that really resonated with those of us from the Pampas, a region the hand of God had created naturally devoid of trees but not of pasture or fertile soil.

―◇―

I returned to town at noon, accompanied by Isidore. Lucía was waiting for me and, delighted that she had accomplished her mission, didn't bother to ask where I had gone.

"My friends are coming this evening. They want to meet you," she announced. "I also made an appointment for you after lunch with Mr. Roberto from the cultural committee. He'll be waiting in his office today at two."

The sky was overcast. Expecting rain, Lucía lent me an umbrella and shortly before 2 p.m. she accompanied me to the town hall.

A path festooned with a kind of pot-bellied tree, the *palo borracho* or *drunkard tree*, led up to the entrance. An early flowering lapacho announced the coming season. Lucía told me that they had celebrated

National Tree Day two days earlier, which explained the garlands still hanging from the branches. The doorman opened the door for me and led me to the office. I was expecting a middle-aged man, but this one wasn't even thirty.

We got right to the point and I told him about the cultural project. The orchestra would give a concert and then invite the children on stage to learn about each instrument. The teachers would be recruited from those musicians in the province who could travel every week.

I was very excited about the program, and even more so because I would have a say in the way music was taught.

"This will be great for our reconstruction plans," the man said. He told me about several of the town's ventures, always placing himself at the center of gravity, with the awareness of someone who feels part of a select vintage. He made it clear that he was not just a municipal employee. Then he added some smarmy words about my talent (of which he knew nothing) and my mission. He asked me if the instrument I played was like a saxophone. I explained to him that the oboe was not made of metal but belonged to the "woodwind family."

"And speaking of wood," I said, "I understand that it was exceedingly difficult for Tartagal when La Forestal abandoned the area, leaving so many people without jobs. Is that right?"

"Yes. Now we have to apply ourselves to attracting other industries, rebuilding the houses that were left empty, and attracting people from outside, people with an entrepreneurial drive who are more educated, like you. And more grateful too."

I asked him what he meant.

"Many people here were employed, for decades, and they had everything. La Forestal provided housing, electricity, running water, public health... all for free. They didn't have to pay for a thing! And yet they still complained."

And I, who have always had a gift—if I can call it that—for saying what's controversial, took aim. "I heard some of them paid with their lives."

His face hardened. "You've probably been talking to one of those urban anarchists who know nothing about our situation."

Suddenly the guy began to address me informally, shifting from *usted* to *tú*. I wasn't bothered by the change but rather by his superior tone: *What did I know?* I told him a few more home truths. Things were going from bad to worse, so I changed the subject. We scheduled some dates for the concert and after a while ended our meeting.

"How long are you staying?" he asked.

"I'm leaving Monday."

"Well, if you have time, I'll pick you up at Lucía's tomorrow, take you to lunch and show you around."

It seemed like a conciliatory gesture, something I never reject. Nobody is perfect. Besides, it would be an opportunity to get back in his good graces.

"That's a good idea," I said, "but first I have to move my things to a hotel because Lucía's husband gets back tomorrow and there's no room for me at the house. They told me about a hostel on 31st Street."

"Sure, it's the only one in Tartagal! It used to be La Forestal's railway station, which is no longer in use of course. We remodeled it to serve as a hostel for the business representatives who sometimes visit us."

"Interesting... They also converted the station in my hometown, but into a museum rather than a hotel. They didn't make many changes, by the way."

"We didn't invest much either, simply built a corridor outside and modernized the bathroom, that's all."

"I think it's the fate of so many of our village train stations to be converted," I commented. "It's a pity how the Argentine Railroad Company has gone into such steep decline."

"Times change and you have to adapt. Well then, tomorrow I'll take you to the hostel. It's too far to go on foot with a suitcase."

I accepted without a moment's thought.

—◇—

Felicia was back preparing dinner. Lucía had invited some of the women from Catholic Action, who greeted me with enthusiastic declarations of friendship. They came dressed their best, most expensive clothes, and what's more with gold dripping from their ears, necks, and arms. It would have put Atahualpa to shame. When I told them I was going to have lunch with Roberto next day, their comments came thick and fast.

"Let's see if you can hook a husband here… He would be a good catch —the Torrentino family owns half the town."

"And how did they become owners? Didn't the town belong to the tannin company?" I asked.

"His grandfather made money off them, and then there were arrangements with the English owners, and in no time they made a fortune."

Felicia, who apparently had been listening, came up to me and said quietly, "Miss, watch out for coral snakes out there."

"But Felicia, I'm going to a restaurant not hunting in the bush!"

The women burst out laughing. She lowered her head.

That night, while I-won't-hear-of-it was sleeping peacefully, I weighed my doubts. On the one hand—and not the best—I was interested in spending some time with this influential guy. On the other hand, I felt I was betraying my principles. I told myself that if I could cultivate a friendlier relationship and manage to bite my tongue, it would benefit the cultural project. Diplomacy is diplomacy! Of course, there are always plenty of arguments that muddy the ethical limits we impose on ourselves.

I slept finally and dreamed of the ancient forests of Chaco, where I wandered lost among the ghosts of trees.

The following diary entry, for no apparent reason, was inserted out of order and written in the present tense. I've transcribed it here, as follows:

Twisted rust. Tanks of tannin, of tree sap, of the blood of men. On a brick wall, red words framed in a wreath of flowers painted with sap and blood. I walk over and read:

To the fallen brothers
Labor movement 1921

I swear that if I get out of this hell, I'll quit and go back home. What if things go wrong for me? Or if I cannot get out at all? I have to get to town. Hopefully this road leads to town... Hopefully the gate is open...

Roberto Torrentino came to pick me up rather late, well after lunchtime. I said my goodbyes to Lucía and Felicia and got into the car with my suitcase. He was driving a red Alfa Romeo, a luxury inconceivable in a town just rising from the ashes. Its owner was not very communicative that morning. Or perhaps what he said lacked the ornamental rhetoric he had used on me the day before? Could it be because of my outfit? My jeans and my tennis shoes? Was I dressed too inelegantly to accompany such a distinguished icon of refined taste?

The hostel was about ten minutes away, but given the size of the town, it could be said that it was located on the outskirts. It occupied an abandoned building facing the railroad tracks, which—just as I expected—was rectangular and single storied. It had a sloping roof, a long colonnaded gallery that had been the station platform, and a wide entrance. A bronze bell, once used to announce the arrival or departure of trains, still hung from a beam in the gallery. This station, or hostel, or whatever you wanted to call it, had the same architecture as all the train stations built by the British in Argentina in the mid-nineteenth century—all had been based on a single blueprint. I could have drawn the plan myself, inch by inch. Not for nothing had I spent my childhood playing with friends in an identical train station in my hometown.

The storm was brewing, its dark clouds riding on top of each other. The Santa Rosa squall was barely a day behind schedule. At any moment it would be unleashed, with the usual theatrical lightning and dramatic flashes.

We entered the waiting room and ticket office, now the hotel lobby. The long polished wooden benches for past travelers, were also familiar. I went up to reception and asked for a room, just for the night. Roberto approached the concierge and said, "Double bed."

"No, I don't need a double—not for just me!" I replied naively.

"Double bed," he insisted, in a self-important tone, without looking at me.

"Yes, Mr. Roberto, as you wish," the concierge said, with the customary kowtowing of the subordinate.

All my alarm bells went off. A chemical reaction began to burn inside me and a rush of blood shot to my face. *Watch out for coral snakes*, Felicia had said. Too late I understood her warning, full of omens! It was obvious to me now that Roberto was the hostel's owner and the concierge his employee. Roberto grabbed my wrist hard. I saw him gesture at the concierge, who closed the lobby's back and front doors. I was paralyzed.

From the ranks of material progress and moral regression, the man who now had me cornered had acquired not only money and power but immunity. And now the wealth-and-power equation was digging its claws into me.

I knew my situation would be impossible to resolve through physical resistance, screaming, the threat of scandal, or begging. My only option was to figure out how to make the circumstances the least traumatic possible. Part of me wanted to show him my contempt, my revulsion. I should have spat in his face. Another part insisted on denying him the pleasure of seeing me reduced to tears and useless supplications, of believing he controlled me at his whim, that his will would be done. What if I had wished for this encounter? Maybe I could manipulate him into thinking so. It would not be a solution but it might ease the situation.

I decided to test the psychological terrain and began by resting my free hand on his. "You rogue! That double bed is not a bad idea," I said, putting on a sly front. "But don't grab so hard—it hurts. Hey, I'm not going to run away!" And going up to his ear, I added, "Could you be a little more romantic? So we can enjoy our time together?" I added this last bit with a seductive smile. Yes, it was a disgusting tactic, but I had to soften him up so he would lower his guard.

As I expected, he shot me a puzzled look. I even laughed at his pathetic expression, which said it all. *What! Won't you resist? You mean I don't have you under my thumb?*

I kept smiling, undaunted. I knew that collaborating with the enemy had its risks. But I would invent something to humiliate him when the time came.

"Marco," he ordered to another employee, "take the lady's suitcase"

"No, I'd rather take it myself," I replied. Of all the absurd ideas that had occurred to me, I had chosen one. Addressing my abductor, I said, "My luggage contains my most precious and only valuable possession. I didn't have time to put the oboe in its case. Such a fragile instrument. I never part with it for that reason."

"Don't worry, Miss, I'll be very careful," said Marco.

We followed him down a dim corridor. To the right there were three doors, the same tall, heavy doors at "my" train station, which would have opened directly onto the platform before the addition of the corridor.

The hotel clerk opened the second door for us and carefully deposited my suitcase in a corner. The window was open and heavy, ozone-laden air was blowing in. Beyond a fledgling forest, not far away, I could see the silhouette of the iconic chimney.

I made a show of putting my purse on the bed and asked about the bathroom.

"At the end of the corridor, Miss," the clerk explained. I already knew this. They had added only the corridor to the original plan; it passed the bathroom and then turned right. At the end, adjacent to the facilities, would be the old pantry.

"Thanks, Marco," I said, and since the Roberto had already let go of me, I slipped between them.

"I'll be right back," I said, heading for the bathroom and forcing myself to walk at a measured pace.

"Is there anything else you need, Mr. Roberto?" asked the clerk.

"No, nothing, Marco," he answered. The employee left and the "coral snake" stood in front of the door, vigilant. He didn't have to. The only way out of the building was through the lobby, in the opposite direction, and even if I turned around and went that way, the concierge wasn't going to take pity on me and unlock the entrance.

I went into the bathroom and locked the door. I saw they had torn down the wall that divided the Ladies and the Gentlemen to make a larger, modern restroom. I climbed on the toilet and then onto the water tank, opening the small window under the ceiling and squeezing through the narrow opening. With half my body hanging out, the truth hit me. I couldn't slide head down. I would smash my skull on the ground. I thought, *better raped than dead*, and gave up.

My plan had failed. Hope shattered, I sat on the toilet, heart pounding like a time bomb, and forced my breath to slow down. What other ideas did I have up my sleeve? I turned on the shower and let it run.

Thunder shook the sky, and I saw a flash of lightning through the small window. In an instant, the gale brought with it the first downpour, a heavy, noisy, crashing on the zinc roof. The electric shock triggered my brain circuits and I imagined other scenes, all improbable, at supersonic speed.

I opened the door a crack and stuck my head out. My nemesis was in the hallway, still stupidly standing guard and staring at the bathroom entryway.

"Hurry, close the window in the room, Roberto! Everything is going to get wet!" I yelled in a bossy tone, playing the part of a domineering wife. Or mother.

The guy was plenty mean but had zero perception or insight. He obeyed like a sheep; no, like a robot. And I took my chance.

I kept the shower running. It took me ten seconds to get out of the bathroom and close the door behind me, to round the corner of the corridor and, following my mental map, find the other door that led to the room behind the two old bathrooms. It was still a working pantry. I opened the window and jumped outside.

I ran, and fear ran with me. I ran like a deer, in the torrential rain, pushed by the wind, leaving behind my purse, my suitcase (I lied, I had not brought the oboe), while the so-called cultural representative of the town of Tartagal waited for me in vain. He would be certain that a musician would not abandon her instrument, nor a woman her purse, and even less so during a storm and from behind a locked door.

It was pouring rain, and I ran across a flat field dotted with stumps and bushes that quickly turned into a sparse forest that became denser the more I ran. I zigzagged through the sturdy trees, sometimes tripping over the roots, and sometimes over my own fears.

By now, I dared to imagine the Idiot would have breached the bathroom, checked the reception area, and returned to the dead-end corridor. When he happened to go into the pantry, he would have seen the open window and, as he looked out onto the vacant lot, a deluge of biblical proportions. Beyond that he would hardly envisage a thorny little forest where I could be found only if they sent out a party of hunting dogs. But no dogs were around. Just him, the mad one.

I came to a stream that had been brought back to life by the Santa Rosa, its surface bristled in the downpour. I found a place to ford the creek and continued running, closely avoiding a face-to-face encounter with a rough wall that suddenly loomed in front of me. It was a three-story brick building, with a profusion of windows but no roof, from which rose the omnipresent chimney, a blurry presence in the rain.

I found myself at the ruins of the Quebracho Argentina, which I entered, out of breath, through a small door.

—◦—

The words I write here can never do justice to the setting. I know that. A mechanical, lifeless, rust-covered world. Aging machinery, wheels, presses, fallen logs, all abandoned like war cannons, mountains of coal, furnaces, circular tanks full of thick rusty liquid, numerous pipes dripping corrosive water. I walked for a while, sheltered from the storm by roofs that were still intact. Although shivering from cold and overwhelmed by the deafening roar of the rain on the metal sheets, I felt safe among those iron mastodons. Amid all the rust, nature was struggling to triumph over the decrepit monstrosity, crawling with its green fingers over the winches, the straps, the mossy concrete pools where once wood was boiled. Life and death together in a covenant of resurrection. Each corner of corroded metal served as a shelter for birds and their nests, protected from their ominous enemy--the storm of the Peruvian saint.

I could see, framed by an inner wall, a door that led to a staircase, made of iron like everything else. I climbed to the second floor. Cautiously, I leaned out of a window with broken and missing glass and took in the tannin factory, a festering scab in the middle of a plain that was once a noble, ancient forest. I tried another window facing east. Yet despite my advantageous position, the curtain of water blocked my view of the station-turned-hotel, or the cultural representative's car, or the guy himself. I saw a lightning bolt snaking through the sky and cracking its whip on the open field I had crossed a few minutes ago. And then the thunder, which shook the air and made the already broken glass quiver.

I thanked *Santa Rosa de Lima* and Nature—her ally and now mine—for a magnificent spectacle. I couldn't picture that wimp of a man venturing out during a thunderstorm. As my imagination ran wild, I saw him run into the parking lot, slip in the mud, fall on his ass, swear, get in the car, and drive off at a suicidal speed. It was a scene conceived only by wishful thinking.

The cry of a *benteveo* bird alerted me and broke up the reverie.

From above, I saw what looked like a scrapyard in front of the factory full of abandoned machinery that resembled dinosaur skeletons and then the main gate. I took note of the dinosaurs as reference points so as not to get lost in the labyrinth. I hurried back down.

As I moved among the ruins, raindrops seeped through the holes in the roof and hit the machines with peculiar metallic sounds—some high, some low, some like timpani, others like cymbals in a percussionist ensemble typical of a Shostakovich piece. This could have been the roar of the tannin factory working, I thought, as I visualized the men sweating while grinding the logs to distill the quebracho's bitter sap.

The rain stopped abruptly. As if it had been my protector, the absence of its commotion seemed threatening to me, and the flapping of each bird was startling. I could not explain why. Silence has sounds that only intuition recognizes and fear magnifies, and its fingers are long reaching.

The sound of footsteps made my blood run cold. They weren't just footsteps, but a rhythmic clanking of chains, as if someone was dragging their shackled feet. I huddled behind a machine. Dread clasped my throat in its suffocating grip. In my confused mental state, I was besieged by ghostly images transmuted into men of flesh, irrational, violent, prowling around an abandoned factory that became a tomb, the tomb of the dead drowned in tannin, or of the living who fled here and were now trapped in a twilight zone. As I was.

I was paralyzed, and all ears. I heard the clicks, and sometimes double-clicks, occasionally followed by short and long whistles. Whoever they were, whether sent by the devil or by the man I could not bear to think about, they were communicating with one another, taking in my presence, because now they could smell my sweat. I was afraid that an uncontrollable groan would escape my throat and give me away.

A gust of wind brought the sounds came closer, along with a rancid smell. I instinctively turned toward the source. A few steps away, a family of tapirs had lined up. And at the end of the line, I saw the young were emerging one by one from a hole in their dark hiding place, their squat round little bodies brushing against a chain that hung over the entrance to their den inside the metal hulk.

The sound of my laughter, my surprise and relief, must have scared them, because they quickly trotted off. I loved them. I wanted to kiss them on their puffy snouts as they sniffed at the air laden with the scents of rain. I joyfully attached myself to the beasts mimicking their double clicks, all of a sudden feeling escorted and safe, unquestionably connected to their tribe through a shared mammalian world. I headed toward the exit with my bodyguards, my mind free of ghosts.

The gate was closed but not locked. It creaked on heavy hinges when I pushed it and stepped out into the open. My tapir friends preferred sneaking out through a hole next to the gate. They went in one direction, following the scent of fresh grass, and I went in another, attracted by the sight of a tall dovecote and, next to it, a humble house.

—<o>—

Smoke from a chimney curled up into the air. In my rush to get there, I paid no attention to where I put my feet. I stepped on a toad, slipped, fell on my back. A cry like a bird's rose from my throat. A dog came up to me, barking, more out of a sense of duty than anger, I think, because he didn't attack. A woman and a child rushed out of the house, alarmed.

Somewhat embarrassed, I got to my feet, and told them I was lost. They saw I was scared and soaked through, and they invited me in.

I don't know how long I remained between those mud walls near the fire trying to recover from the verge of hypothermia, and to quell the adrenaline that had pushed me this far. I shook from head to toe as though there were an engine running under my skin. Uncontrollably trembling, I took off my tennis shoes and put them to dry near the fireplace. The woman offered me a poncho that smelled strongly of smoke. I wrapped myself in it, feeling grateful to those good people from the bottom of my soul.

An older man came out of another room. He was scrawny and looked liverish.

When the chills and chattering had subsided and I was able to speak, my hosts wanted to know how I had gotten there. I told them the truth, including all the details but withholding names.

"Whoever that bastard is, girl, don't worry about it, because if he shows up, we'll send Yaraví to bite him!" they consoled me. Hearing its name, the dog pricked up its ears. Still shaking, I patted him.

We talked quietly for hours. The woman served the man *mate* but gave me "healing tea," which I assumed was made from the bark of the mighty carob tree. I asked them if they had worked in the mills or as loggers, and my questions unleashed a host of stories and emotions. The man recounted his life and the lives of others, and all the various misfortunes visited on them by La Forestal.

"Yes, I was an axman, Miss. What a miserable life! I have seen more than one buddy broken in two, as if by lightning, when the quebracho fell the wrong way and on top of the people below. Others were bitten by the yarará snake—nothing works against its poison. It's a horrible death that … I tell you."

The man spoke with the forcefulness and truth of a troubled soul still suffering from what he had seen. Imaginary ax in hand, he put his whole body into his stories. He said he could still hear the axes pounding in the bush at night. Sensitive to rhythms, I thought I could make them out as well, and the images of a pounding, violent death made my chest tighten.

The former axman's wife, who had been occupied with the *mates*, while keeping the fire alive and me warm, interrupted.

"Some folks in town say that during the time of La Forestal there was luxury. Sure, but the luxury was only for them. We Tobas lived here with snakes, and ticks, and tuberculosis, which took our parents too early, at thirty or thirty-five… Think about it, Miss! We never had those kinds of diseases before. And the kids … they also died on us. We watched them go, one by one, as soon as they were born, or after a year or two. The kids that survived grew up did so by the grace of God, and at eleven they were already felling trees. Those were bad times to be a child."

Her husband nodded, his head and body hunched over. And he added, "They treated us like animals. We Tobas were never *real* people for them. 'Brute Indian!' I remember them yelling at us. Or 'Fucking lazy Indian, move your feet!' Excuse my language, Miss, but that's what they said. No, we were never *people* as far as the foremen or their foreign employers were concerned. Only Indians. Our lives didn't count."

In spite of the intensity, there was also humility here, as if they wanted to be forgiven for the audacity of staying alive. A deep grief and rage overwhelmed me. And I, who have a hard time controlling my emotions, felt my eyes fill with tears. I would have liked to kneel down and ask their forgiveness in the name of my race—if there is such a thing—my skin color, my history, because my predecessors of pure Italian stock are not exempt from guilt. Racism had crossed the Atlantic in ships sailing under every flag.

"And then, when the company left, Miss (I had told them my name, but he preferred using 'Miss'), if you want to know, many of our people left and went to the capital. Some came back because they found nothing there. But we stayed because at least here you can hunt and eat an armadillo now and again."

The younger woman hugged the child, who was looking at me with his huge, still, deep eyes, knowing and not knowing why mine were watery.

I registered the pain—the pain of others also hurts.

The clouds had gathered at the edge of the world, leaving the sky above us clear, and we went out to sit on some logs under a tree. The afternoon saw flocks of birds flying away and pigeons returning home. The shadows stretched themselves out on the damp ground that was grateful for water. And soon, a golden light filtered through torn clouds in a horizon so easily visible in that flat and devastated land, turned our faces the color of the sun. I fully took in the supernatural beauty, so at odds with earthly misery, and that further stirred the sea of emotions that had already overwhelmed me. I wanted to cry.

I had been there for hours, for most of the afternoon. I needed to leave, but I didn't feel like walking back through the desolate place alone, with no idea how to get to town and the threat of coming across the coral snake. Then I saw a cart and a horse under a shed. I didn't have any money on me, of course, but the sunset's golden glow gave me an idea. I removed the gold chain with its medal from around my neck and offered it to the family.

"Would you take me to town? I have no money, but this is worth something."

"No need, Miss. We'll take you without pay."

I appreciated their nobility, but I insisted, and at last we decided that I would keep the medal—a gift from my godmother, who lies peacefully in her grave, as I told them—and the woman of the house would keep the chain. "Women know how to manage money better than men," I added. And everyone laughingly agreed.

They sent the boy to untie the horse and hitch it to the cart. I lay down in the back and covered myself with a tarp in case we ran into an Alfa Romeo on the road. The old man and the boy climbed onto the box seat, and with a *giddyup!* we hurried away. Night was approaching.

We went along roads that were by then full of shadows and as night fell we neared Lucía's house, the only place where they could, and should, receive me. I said goodbye to my benefactors and jumped off the cart at the corner. The toads were copulating under the yellow streetlights. I was gripped by a dizzying nausea.

In a wretched state, I knocked on my hosts' door.

The mayor had already arrived home. I told the couple what had happened. When I finished, they both appeared as unfazed as the ceramic elves that adorned their garden, as if they didn't believe me or didn't want to believe me. But they ended up accepting my story as true—my outrage was obvious—and Lucía's husband apologized. After all, the so-called president of the town's culture committee was a mere subordinate in the municipal hierarchy.

Felicia served me hot soup. She gazed at me with a mixture of admiration and compassion.

Heraldo was more sophisticated than his wife, although he suffered from the same ideological rigidity. He told me a little about Roberto and his family, the Torrentinos. They had benefited from La Forestal's presence for decades, true. But it had to be recognized that the company had brought extraordinary wealth to a poor community in the middle of the Santa Fe's chaco region. He told me about the railroads, the hospitals, the schools. I, having taken in all the hardships I had heard, thought that he was pouring praise on garbage. I pointed out that the railroads had been built to carry the stolen products of the land to the port of Buenos Aires so they could be sent to Europe, and not for the people; that the schools and clinics had been for administrators and foremen, not the Tobas woodcutters, the workers at the wood mills, or their families. Who had all that ancient splendor benefited? And without pausing, I told him about the massacre of the trade unionists. This time I didn't do it to be provocative: I honestly wanted to get to the truth of the matter and it was my way of finding out. It was my natural inclination to try to resolve ambiguities, and I saw this one as exceptionally corrosive.

"But that skirmish with the strikers was fifty years ago!" he answered. By now he was irritated.

"Fifty-one, to be precise. Well, paleolithic shit might be a fossil, but it's still shit, right?" I answered.

Lucía put her hand to her lips. Felicia dropped the ladle with which she was stirring the soup. At that point in my life I was foul-mouthed, and I was slow to remember that I was in an environment that wasn't mine, that provincial folks are always more conservative in their language as in everything else. I apologized and attacked from another flank.

"La Forestal usurped the power of the state, Heraldo. It had its own police force, minted its own coins, passed laws, and acted as judge, court, and prison all at once. You know that."

"Usurped, no, it supplanted! The central government gave them the go-ahead to do whatever they wanted. They sold the region to them and washed their hands of it."

"A deal between swindlers," I retorted.

The mayor didn't reply. The silence told me that the guy no longer knew how to defend his position, and that the screws in his ideological framework were coming loose.

Or maybe that wasn't it. Maybe I didn't deserve his answer. At the end of the day, I was their guest, an ungrateful and mouthy one at that, not to mention impertinent. I had sown something ugly in their nest. Not knowing how to back down, I kept quiet.

It was time to leave. I said goodbye to Felicia, offering my hand, which she took, along with the gold medal tucked between my fingers. She clenched her fist and shoved the prize surreptitiously under her armpit, marching to her room with her arm held tight against her body.

Lucía and her husband drove me to the terminal to catch the night bus to Santa Fe, where I would make a connection to Corrientes. It was the only option I could find to get out of town immediately. They bought my ticket and gave me money for the next bus. Promising to pay them back as soon as I reached my destination, I said goodbye to the woman with whom I had shared a bed for two nights, kissing her on the cheek. Her husband extended his hand, happy to see me gone.

The return trip seemed endless. My mind ran through a nonstop dialogue about the events of those two days. By the time I boarded the second bus, at midnight, I was flushed with fever. In the rare lucid moments fever allow for, I understood the meaning of what had happened, or what could have happened. It was not merely punishment inflicted by my stalker for my political or, rather, ethical position. It was also a message. *We don't want you here, not you nor your music nor your orchestra. We do not want anarchists or communists to repopulate this town. Don't come back.* That's what I understood.

I could justify his monolithic ideology, if I wanted to be caritative, because he had come from the same crass material as his predecessors. But not the sadism of the rapist; that is part of the loathsome material of many men and is unforgivable.

Or is it another of the various faces of a polyhedron? The same multifaceted male desire for power?

I arrived at my rented room early Monday morning. I was extremely ill, with a band of anxieties stretched across my heart.

I called the conductor, resigned from the orchestra, and rescinded the contract "for health reasons." I told him that my mission had failed, that I had not found much interest, and that being a cultural diplomat was too big a job for me. I made a joke about the musicians in the woodwind row in the orchestra—oboes, bassoons, clarinets—about how they were not fit to go to towns where the woods had been squandered and their best product stolen. I suggested he try his luck sending the percussionists. I don't know if he understood. Was it worth telling him what had happened? No, it would be a complaint that would go nowhere. Or worse. To report sexual harassment was to bring shame on myself. The woman was invariably blamed.

Before I left that week, I received a big package sent by the mayor of Tartagal. It contained my suitcase, my purse and, inside, my wallet with everything intact. There was also a small gift for me. It was a necklace made from carob seeds and with a note in large, traced letters that said:

This necklace is an amulet against coral snake bites.
Always grateful, Felicia Aricayá-Nhandutí

I still have it today.

Woodland Park Zoo feline house, 1951.
Engineering Department (Record Series 2613-07), Seattle Municipal Archives.

The Boys of Boise 1955
Alex Vigue

It's the sound of wind kissing
juniper trees in the park,
it's a lighthouse cop
hunting to catch carnality
& bind it in metal

I am conceived in these
circumstances, a fledgling
dribble or spit pine seed,
earth drinker,

semen missed by a stranger
to be consumed by
the shared roots &
mycelium of drag mother nature

pheromones of fear
cruising in Idaho
gnawing at branches,
gnawing at the rule of an unjust law

the men have swallowed
their own arms
and I am born of this fellating,
a child of "Infamous crimes
against nature."

Six years probation
Ten years in prison
Five years in prison
Seven years in prison. Loses
appeal to the Idaho supreme court
Five years in prison
Fifteen years in prison
Five years in prison. Loses
appeal to the Idaho supreme court

Angela Garbes in conversation with Alayna Becker

Spring 2022

If we're ever successful in any kind of revolution, I'm certain it will be in part because of the words and ideas of Angela Garbes. Her book Essential Labor: Mothering for Social Change *came out this year on Mother's Day and has already made a significant cultural impact with her stunning prose and resonate message: we have a massive care problem in the United States. Garbes expands the definition of essential labor to parents and caregivers of all kinds. This work of maintenance, of wiping and washing, cooing and disciplining, of feeding and scrubbing is the labor on which our society actually depends. Mothers deserve more support, care workers, in particular care workers of color, must be paid a wage commensurate with the importance of their work.*

Essential Labor *is a generous invitation to do things differently. To listen to and love our bodies. To dance and sweat and hold each other. To show up, and to be shown up for. To eat and taste every bite. To be honest with the people we love. To show the care workers we depend on solidarity. It's an invitation. Garbes is showing us what we could have: how will we take care of each other?* –AB

Becker

Maybe we can start by talking about abortion, before getting too much into your book itself. You and I were both involved in the anthology *Shout*

Your Abortion, which was published back in 2018. That project pulled me into writing and was so pivotal in my path to embodied work and embodied writing, and I learned so much from you, specifically. It was amazing to go back and reread your essay from that anthology now, almost four years after it came out. There was this line near the end of your essay where you say, "How many stories do the people who care for us hold?" It was just so striking to see there the same thoughts and feelings about caregiving that you're exploring in your new book, *Essential Labor*—to see how that story really centered the provider.

Garbes

Yeah, it's interesting. I did an event recently for this organization called National Advocates for Pregnant Women; they provide on-the-ground legal support for people who are being prosecuted for having miscarried. I was in conversation with this amazing woman named Mimi Niles, who's a midwife, and she talked about how she decided to become a midwife because she had an abortion and she never felt more cared for. She just felt so held, like she never had a health care provider pay that much attention to her… I might start crying.

It was the day we all found out about the leaked Supreme Court opinion in *Dobbs*. We were all crying at the event. They were sort of scrambling, like, how are we going to frame the event? And I was thinking, "I don't know that we need to frame it." You know what I mean? We've been living in this moment for a long time, and I want to hold space for people, but I need to tell that story again, the story of that woman and that abortion care provider.

Thank you for bringing this up, because I hadn't read or even thought about that essay in a while. Care is a thing I have been thinking about for a long time. And it has everything to do with my parents and the work that they did. And then even when I was working primarily as a food writer. To me, food is nourishment, and care is an important aspect of cooking, especially in the home. Home cooking, particularly, has always interested me more than restaurant cooking, despite the fact that I had to write restaurant reviews. It's about how we take care of each other, how we take care of ourselves. I got a little chill when you said that line: "how many stories do the people who care for us hold?" I was thinking of it so specifically in the context of that care provider who I would see out and about after my abortion. And she just never betrayed that confidence. What struck me most of all was that she does this for so many people. Care providers like her are so skilled. It takes so much to do that. I've been thinking about that and her for a long time.

Becker

Yeah, man. When I was a teenager, I took a ceramics class from this woman named Casey, and I didn't know it at the time, but she also worked at Planned Parenthood as a nurse. And then when I went for my abortion, there she was. At first, I was embarrassed. And just like in your case, she met me, and it was like, "Oh, wait, but you're here, right? We're all here. So, it's all fine."

There is just so much generosity on the part of caregivers. It makes me think about the generosity of memoir. In your book, you write into so many areas of your personal life that are, I think, areas for shame in our colonized world of white supremacy. There are all kinds of uncomfortable conversations with your kids and with your community on topics that we aren't supposed to write about. That we aren't even supposed to talk about. There are so many things in this book. And it resonated so deeply. So, my question is this: You could have written a theory book. Like, you could have written a very smart, capital-S, smart ass book, and you wrote

Art, you made art. How does that art-making process intersect with the capital-S smart theory behind it?

Garbes

Thank you for saying that. I think of myself as a creative person, and I know that I'm creating art. I've never really named myself as an artist. For me, writing is certainly creative, but there's also just a component where… I don't know, I think maybe it was that growing up, I was never told it's okay to be an artist. My parents are very supportive, but they were never like, "yes, be an artist." They were like, "you should go to college so that you can get a business degree." You know what I mean? The idea was that I was going to become a professional in some way. First, I had to come to a place where I could think of my writing as a creative outlet for myself. But writing is also an act of service for me. It's very clarifying. I want to write the books and the essays and the pieces that I didn't have growing up. The starting point is, what do I need from this? And writing is certainly where I work out a lot of my thoughts and feelings. Like, how do I know what I think until I write it? One way that I approach this service component of writing is by giving people permission to question the framing of certain things. There's this idea, as you point out, that we're not supposed to talk about certain things. But, says who? Says everyone who wants to control us, everyone who doesn't want us to speak our truth, to be embodied, to feel powerful. And so, a part of that service is rejecting these ideas. There's no shame in being a person. There should not be shame attached to that. There *should* be shame attached, I think, to deliberately hurt someone, though, right? But I don't really think there's anything else in the human existence that is deserving of shame. This is something that I've been growing into and learning as I've gotten older.

But the thing I will say is this: the idea of writing a capital-S smart book is scary. For most of my life, my biggest fear has been that someone would meet me and think I wasn't smart, because the way I was raised, there was a sense that you had to prove your value as a person of color. My parents are immigrants. To be smart was to be useful, to be valuable, to be assimilated—and thus legible to white people. And I think deep down inside I doubted whether that path was really for me, but you just sort of do as you're told, and you learn what's modeled for you. At the same time, I always had this part of me that felt wilder and sort of shadowy—and probably a little scary to my parents. I didn't really understand it. Even though I was getting straight As in school and really trying to succeed, there was part of me inside that was always asking, "So why are we Catholic?"

Or I would ask my parents things like, "Can you explain colonialism to me?" And they were like, "What are you talking about? Why do you care? This is just who we are, all right?" But I had all these other questions.

So writing was not a thing that I thought I could do for a living. I knew I was good at it, and that I liked it. But that doesn't mean… you know, how many people swallow their dreams? My parents did that. You know what I mean? They came here. They were essentially forced here for economic reasons. I don't think they got to really be the people they wanted to be. And so, I was like, "Why would I get to be the person that I really wanted to be?" Love is sacrifice. Life is hard. You don't get to do all those things. I has this sense that I wasn't entitled to my dreams necessarily. Later, when I started getting opportunities to write professionally, it was mostly food writing, which was very servicey, very practical. But being legible and smart and eloquent is something that's always been important to me. And as I've gotten older and become more comfortable with myself, that inner part of me that is like, "I am a human animal who just wants to eat all the time and lay around and touch people and sweat on them and roll around."

I've just become much less interested in hiding, and much more interested in cultivating and nurturing that person. Becoming a mother just physically opened me in a way—and after that, I couldn't deny that I was a body, an animal. And so, to think about writing a book that was purely intellectual, all research and theory, seemed at odds with that identity. I love everything I do at this point, and maybe it's internalized whiteness, but now, at almost 45, I can't fundamentally change who I am. But speaking of internalized whiteness, there's this other feeling, too. I never would have guessed that I would write memoir. The idea is something that I was always really afraid of. Even though I believed in my inherent value as a person, and in the importance of my story, I never thought that other people would be interested. Like, memoirs are for white ladies, right? Who have anorexia or who went to Paris and figured out food and love or something. I just felt like: if I'm going to write a book, if I'm going to tell my story, I have to make it useful to people.

I'm opening an emotional portal by telling you about something that happened in my life, but I'm not doing that because I think my story is more important than yours. I'm telling you because I'm trying to create an access point where you can slip in, and then I'm like, "So let me tell you about the statistics of domestic laborers and how bad their wages are." It's just how my mind works. No one teaches you this as a genre. This is just where I feel most comfortable. This is the best use of my talents, and my desire to be of service—the best use of storytelling.

Becker

Yes.

Garbes

I think about Filipino American women like myself, and in some ways, what I want to do is give us all permission to tell our stories however we want to tell them. That's a long answer, but I guess that's what we're here for.

Becker

Well, as you've been talking about desire and specifically the idea of following your desire in writing, it makes me think of the way you talk about the body. I mean, this whole book is about the body and embodiment. It's about how alienation from the body is what makes capitalism possible. And the only way to halt it is for everybody to wake up in their bodies because your body simply cannot be against desire. I really love how, early on in the book, you bring in Audre Lorde's definition of the erotic. "We tend to think of the erotic as an easy, tantalizing sexual arousal," Lorde writes. "I speak of the erotic as the deepest life force, a force which moves us toward living in a fundamental way."

I'm curious about how embodiment influenced your actual practice of writing. And then there's the relinquishing of control that you talk about in parenting, the idea of creating more space for things to go wrong or for uncomfortable things to be said. How have those two areas had an impact on your writing practice?

Garbes

I'm going to start with this idea of letting go. For so many of us, one thing that causes a lot of misery in life is feeling like you're not living up to some sort of standard. And I think I knew from an early age that I was never going to meet anyone's idea of what, like, a "good girl" was. I was never going to meet the idea of what a fine, upstanding young woman was. And a lot of that has to do with whiteness.

But also, a lot of other things. I was never going to meet the standard of what a "good mother" was. There has been pain and grief in processing that. But also, there has been a tremendous amount of freedom. And what I realized, I think, is that marginalized people are more in touch with this idea. I think sometimes for white people, it's harder because you're closer to that standard. And so, you could spend your whole life almost getting there. Whereas for a lot of us, we're like, "Well, fuck it. We're never going to be that. So, what do I want to be?" That realization can come with some turmoil. But another goal of this book is, I just want people to let go of any idea of an ideal person or ideal mother, ideal caregiver, ideal daughter, ideal any kind of person. Because if we let go of that, we could just freely be the people that we are. That idea is so beautiful to me.

Because perfection is just so unrealistic. It's not what people are. Humans are so messy. We fuck up all the time. By focusing on perfection, we're just setting ourselves up to feel terrible all the time. And that's not to say you shouldn't work to improve yourself. But we'd feel so much happier if we were pursuing ourselves as opposed to some ideal. We could just be us. And in parenting specifically, like, mistakes will be made. There's no way around that. What I'd rather do is make the mistake and come to my children and tell them, like, "I'm sorry. I'm sorry. Mommy was thinking about something else entirely. And that's why I yelled at you, because I was feeling sad about something else." In the last few years, especially, there's been so much of that because we're all just in this pressure cooker, and there was no place to get away. There was no place to process. I mean, I was clinically depressed, and I couldn't go be social. I couldn't go do things.

It was all happening in my home. One way of coping was by trying to hide myself. And in some ways, I'm a master of trying to hide myself from even the people who know and love me the best. But it made so much more sense to be who I was and talk to them about it. Because then also, by doing that, I'm modeling what wasn't modeled for me. There's a song by Melissa Manchester called "Don't Cry Out Loud." Do you know it? It's this 80s song, and it goes, "Don't cry out loud. Just keep it inside." I was told to not have emotions. And I realized like, oh, this is an opportunity for me, too. One thing you'll find a lot of in this book is me mothering myself. And it's not because it's not because my mom failed at anything. It's because my mom is a human being who had her own needs and couldn't provide me everything. There's no way that I can provide everything for my children. I know that no matter what I do, mistakes will be made, and they'll probably have something to talk about with me when I'm older. But there was so much silence and suppression in my family, and that was also, in a way, their cultural inheritance. A lot of this book is me trying to understand that, but I want to model those things, so my children won't have to learn that on their own. I want them to see me having emotions and see me processing those emotions so they will feel free to do that. I want them to know that they can talk to me about anything. We have so little control over things.

So, all of this has been a great thing that's happened, especially since, like, my mid-30s, before I had kids: I've just been sort of letting go of this need to control everything. It still shows up in a lot of ways. The other part of that question, which I love, too, is about the physicality of writing as work. I have spent so much time thinking about writing as a physical practice because, until I have a final product, there's a voice in my head that's, like, "all you're doing is sitting on your ass. You're just sitting here having your little thoughts—your stupid fucking life of the mind—when there are people out there doing actual work, actual physical labor, which is so much harder and so much more draining.

It was dance that really helped me to see this from a new perspective. I would step into a dance space—a studio, a dance floor—and it was very strange. I was doing things just for me. And people seemed drawn to me. People seemed appreciative of my energy. At the same time, I also felt like I was working so much shit out that talking could never do—and that writing could never do. I could feel that I was communicating with people and forging a closeness with them. And none of it fit into the rubric of what I understood communication to be. That dance practice and movement practice really brought me into a deeper relationship with my body where I can listen to it, where I'm thematically clued into my feelings. When I have a feeling now, I feel it in my body more, or I'm at least cultivating an understanding of that. And so part of that, too, has been thinking a lot about how to make writing a physically pleasurable practice for me. I haven't figured it out yet.

For one thing, I move a lot more in my space. I take breaks. I walk around. I sometimes walk around with my phone or type little notes. And so, I try to encourage ideas to happen by physically moving my body. I mean, it's true that there's no escaping sitting down and having to do that. There are people like Melissa Broder, who wrote *The Pisces*, who write on their phones or through dictation. But like, I can't. I like the idea of that, but that's not going to be me. I've tried to engage my body more in my practice of writing. But the way the physical pleasure of writing has shown up more is that I'm thinking about it as a reader. I read my book aloud to myself multiple times during the editing process. I don't want to privilege the mind over the body. That's what I think we're taught to do.

I'm just figuring it out. I'm fucking around because I don't know the answer to this. But I've been trying to find a way to have both mind and body be present. In my own writing, my goal has been to make the body undeniable, so that when you're reading it, you have physical sensation—so that you might feel some of those things in your body. I've been making a list of personal words that I feel in my body when I read—and that I think other people might feel in that way, too. And this is something that stems, in a way, from when I was working as a food writer. I used to get beautiful feedback from people who said, "When I read your articles, at some point, I feel the physical experience of eating, or at least some aspects of that." I've been trying to figure out how to translate physical experience into language. I love that you ask that question, because it's totally something that I'm actively trying to do.

Becker

Same, actually, which is why I ask. Right before the pandemic, I took a modern dance class for the first time, thinking it would be, like, hip hop. But instead, they were like, "What does your body want to do?" And I was like, "Oh, shit. I have no idea." I'm still looking into finding out what that is. It reminds me of the way you write about all of this in the "Mothering Toward Movement" chapter of your book. You just bring so much to the writing. And it is so clear throughout this whole book that it is focused so intently on the body. In this chapter, you write a lot about food. The way you write about food is healing, to give that much love and reverence to building scenes around food where the table is full in this chapter. It is a fully sensual experience of food.

Garbes

Yeah. Which is what food is. It's a sensual experience. It's a physical experience. It engages with multiple senses. I feel like I was in touch with some kind of magic when I was writing that chapter—it made me so happy because I haven't been writing about food for the last few years. And it really is sort of like my first love. It's what brought me into writing—the food I grew up with and that I love so deeply. Food also for a long time was my strongest connection to my cultural identity. I wanted to lovingly paint those pictures and let myself do that because no one else was going to give me the space to do it. I had to make that space for myself, and it made me so happy. It was a deeply emotional experience. "Healing" is a good word. This book, to me, is healing. But that chapter, in particular, was very pleasurable. It's really me making sense of so many things in my life that I've been grappling with, like appetite, identity, and pleasure. All of these things are really tied up in a way that I don't think I fully understand yet, but I was just trying to unbraid them and re-braid them in a way that made sense to me.

Becker

Yeah, absolutely. Food is also so interesting in the context of American empire, because for an empire, food is a matter of great importance. "We need all these workers. We need all these bodies doing labor, and we need to feed them all as cheaply as possible." And I think that sort of mentality really cleaves the physical experience you're talking about from one's relationship with food. It becomes, as you say, a matter of efficiency, eating for efficiency. You talk about eating 50% Filipino food and 50% American growing up.

Garbes

Yeah. And that was a great split, you know what I mean? It saved my mom and dad's asses. My mom, sometimes she'll talk about Hamburger Helper, and she gets this sort of feeling about it as her helper. I think as someone who was working full time and raising three kids, she needed a helper. She fucking loved Hamburger Helper. I think she also liked it when we ordered pizza.

But to tie this back to the idea of domestic labor—as I was recently saying to my husband, we are not meant to cook three meals a day, seven days a week. On top of our jobs. You just can't do it. We have a little more money these days and we've had for a while so it's okay for us to get takeout because we're not meant to cook all those meals. Like, it's okay for us to have the Mandarin Orange chicken from Trader Joe's. I know they don't allow unions, but we're going to do it. I know there's no ethical consumption under capitalism, but it's okay because I'll lose my mind if we don't. The other interesting thing is that when I first met my husband, he was totally the kind of person who was like, "I just eat for calories. I just eat so I can get through the day." And I was like, "I am so sorry." I didn't understand that at all. But at the time, I didn't know that he grew up basically on welfare.

And his mom—this is amazing—she used to place bulk orders for food. She would call, like, Sysco—you know, the wholesale restaurant food distributor? She would place quarterly orders for things like the deli meat that was sliced really thin. And she would have it rationed out, like down to individual Ham sandwiches. So first of all, I think about the tremendous amount of labor, and especially mental labor, that went into doing that. But then also, that's just a very different way of eating. I was so fortunate to grow up eating the way that I did. And then he is still affected by that experience in some ways. And I am too, actually. I've learned from him, for example, that not every meal has to be a long, sensual experience. Sometimes, I just need to shove egg roll in my mouth. But it's a balance. I don't know. I'm going to stop talking because I feel like you have a better question than what I'm going to say now.

Becker

I just can't imagine that's true. I wrote down questions earlier and now they just completely don't exist anymore.

Garbes

We're just talking.

Becker

We're just talking about all these things like food and eating, mothering as encouraging appetites. It is like such an inheritance from our mothers, our relationships to our bodies. And I just so completely relate to what you experienced as your inheritance from your mother, your relationship to your body. And having a mother who is smaller than you, which I also have.

Garbes

Yeah. I can feel like there are certain things about how this resonates with you. And you don't have to include this if you don't want to but I would love to dig into that a little bit more. The first reader for my book was Jen Graves, who used to be the arts writer for *The Stranger*. She and I have remained really close friends. But as she was reading, she would say things like, "you need to pull out this moment." And I didn't realize it at the time, but of course, I was thinking of my pain as *my own personal pain*. I think a lot of women have this feeling of, "where did I come from?" And I really thought it was just me. But Jen—she was like, "no, it's not just you." She said, "I think you need to give that space because it's going to hit people in different ways." And so I wonder if you wouldn't mind telling me a little more about that. Is that what you felt? Like, "who am I? How do I place myself in the world if I can't see myself in this person whose body I literally came from?"

Becker

This is so interesting because it has been an issue for me recently in a way that it hasn't been maybe in a few years. Partially because my body has been changing, and I've been struggling to kind of reconcile those changes with myself—and then there's also being closer to my mom, who's a nurse, and smaller than me, so a lot of her language around the body is very clinical, and can feel like facts about "how it's supposed to be" or "how you're supposed to eat." I mean, I have a memory from when I was ten years old, and I was eating an Easy Mac. This is a painful memory. And she came in and was like, "you need to stop eating that or you will get fat." And in retrospect, I look at that moment and know it wasn't about me. She was repeating what she had been told, what she told herself. She was repeating something that I can now choose to accept or not.

But to get back to the book, part of the remodeling process for me is like finding my own truth and my own narrative. So, what of this inheritance is fact? And what do I get to choose for myself? Do I get to choose to be happy in my body? Because that feeling of fatness is like, "oh, then I am unlovable." Like, active people will see that you're less healthy. We all know what fat phobia is, right? But it's also couched in health, and becomes a form of moral policing, but under the guise of health.

Garbes

Absolutely. Yeah.

Becker

And just none of it—simply none of it—is real. My body and brain are kind of like working on making my version of truth in my body the one truth I feel.

Garbes

Thank you for sharing that. I also want to be clear: the ending of that chapter is a way of saying, "I'm still working on it." I am very much working on it. I feel like I've come to a place—and I had already gotten to this place before I had children—where I like my body. But then I was like, "oh, let me just fucking destroy my body, change it in every possible way, and have no real control over what it's going to look like. Oh, and then let me do it again." I've been on this journey working to get to a place of acceptance. It's not even, like, full on love, but just acceptance and neutrality. And then what's really hard is, once you get there and you realize, like, "oh, I don't get to stop doing this for the rest of my life. I don't get to take the rest of my life off. I have to keep doing this." And that's really, like… I'm tired. Do I get nothing? No props, no points? In another part of this book, I talk about the satisfaction of taking care of yourself. It is work, but it's the work that really matters. More and more, I feel that investing in myself is going to pay dividends I can't even begin to see yet. I don't think I'm ever going to regret it. I know I'm never going to regret it.

At the same time, I want to be really clear in this book that, like, yes, I have some thoughts, which I am sharing. I have some ideas toward an ethics of care and some values that we should be centering or recentering. But I'm not saying, "you should do this." It's not as though I've figured something out. I think this book dwells a lot more, especially its second half, on questions rather than answers.

Becker

I think the generosity of memoir—both generally, and in this specific instance—is that it's in no way prescriptive. It is an invitation to engage with the same questions you're grappling with. And it feels that way the whole way through.

Garbes

Good. I like that it feels like an invitation. That's right. That feels right to me.

Becker

I want to read this quote because it is so stunning. You're talking about doing physical care labor, and you have this incredibly beautiful line about your initial resistance to doing the thing because you're being taken away from something else, your work, your time, and the physical work becomes sort of a meditation. I'm going to read it to you, I guess.

Garbes

Okay. No, great. It's fun. You don't often get to hear other people read your words to you.

Becker

"It is draining, tedious, and repetitive, but the work keeps us close to one another, returns us, again and again, to our own corporeal forms. Physical labor exhausts me, but it makes me more tender. More empathetic, more sensate, more porous. In touch with all the emotions."

So that really feels like a devotional, even just like a living, physical devotion meditation of love, of your community and family.

Garbes

Yeah. I know I wrote them, but the two parts in there that jumped out to me are, "more sensate" and "more porous." I feel like I wouldn't have been able to write that five years ago. I don't fear a sort of overwhelming sensation anymore, because now I have better tools, like the ability to ask myself, "what am I feeling?" That porousness is so beautiful. Like, when you feel yourself to be permeable to other people and you feel the power that you physically have to affect each other and comfort each other without words, that's some of the most beautiful shit out there, to me. That's what life is for. I could just hold the people that I love. I can hold them for hours. That's what I want to do all the time.

Especially coming out of the pandemic when we were all so divorced from one another. I don't want to police myself, but I have definitely been in situations where I saw this guy, like, at a protest, and he was a very handsome guy. It's not like I had a thing for him. But like, I just kept touching him. I was like, "How are you? Oh, my God. I touched his beard, and I was like, "What are you fucking doing?" to myself.

This is unhinged, but I just wanted to touch people. I have missed that. And I have thankfully not gotten tired of touching. At times, I felt exhausted by my children and my husband—well, actually not by my husband. I felt dead inside for a long time to the extent that when I did experience touch, I felt nothing. It wasn't enough. You know what I mean? And that's again where I missed dance. I missed bumping into people in a bar, incidental contact. I realized that a lot of how I satisfied some of my big desire to be physically close to people had been just being in crowded places. That's just part of life, and when that went away, I felt that I was missing a huge part of my life. Going back to that quote, though—to be fair, it's about labor, and that's what care work is fundamentally about. It's the inescapability of the body. Even if we're not talking about care or mothering or children, it's just what you have to do as a person.

Like, if you don't, you have to take a shower eventually, right? You have to feed yourself. You'll have to cut your nails. And that's all that stuff that we're not supposed to talk about, but it's so important. It's the only work you can't get away from. While writing this book, something that's been so clear to me is that care is the work of humans. Care is the only real work. I don't need to have a job. I need to keep myself alive, to define myself outside of work and to fully inhabit my body. I think that's like a challenge for a lot of people. It's a challenge for me.

Becker

To go back to our parents, your mother sounds very similar to my mother—the way they learned to survive under these challenges. And my mother in particular, she believed that her shortcomings were her fault. That's the power of those narratives.

Garbes

Yes. And I think that that's true of a lot of women—especially women of certain generations, like, boomers, I guess. I don't know how old your mother is, but I feel like there was the civil rights movement and all of that hippie shit. Like, that happened for some people, but it also didn't happen. That was counterculture. Just as many women of that generation had a different experience, of trying to "have it all"—have a job, have a family, do all these things to seek fulfillment, take care of everyone else, show your love through sacrifice and being of service to other people. Yeah. I have a deep empathy for that because it's so fucked up. And I feel really fortunate that I grew up knowing that there were more options.

Becker

This might be my last question, but I really want to talk about the second to last chapter, the chapter about sex. This is another instance where your writing is just phenomenal. I'm obsessed with the passage where you talk about making out when you're 14 and trying to extend that experience of desire without a specific end in mind. I totally know what you're talking about. You then dive into a scene where you are camping with your husband without kids. The scene is stunning and unlike any sex scene I've ever read. I'll quote you here, "It had been a long time since we had just touched each other for a sustained period of time, without knowing almost exactly what would happen. Hours were lost on that blanket, and my skin felt fuzzy, like the polar friction between two magnets that are attracted, in relationship, though they won't quite come together." The scene extends into unscripted intimacy. "We converged on that trip, but something broke too: any preconceived notion of what might happen, what should happen. There was only the moment, only the universe and warmth that happened as we touched, we were swimming in it, coming up for air, diving back into it, floating on our backs, treading—did it matter, really, where we were going or where we would end up?"

And I think it is so important and true that we think of sex as a means to an end in our culture. That's what it is designed as. I guess I would love to hear from you about the process of writing that chapter, because nobody's ever done that before.

Garbes

Yeah. I guess I'll start by saying that in my mind, when I decided I was going to write a chapter on sex, I wanted it to be mainly about the sex education system in America and how only, like, 14 states require sex ed to be medically accurate, and how it's all preventive. Then I was starting to write, and I realized, "well, I've played myself again." There was no way that was going to be it, because... I'm me. And the way I write necessarily means that I'm going to have to talk about myself. I avoided it for a long time. And then I was doing this thing. This relates to something you mentioned earlier, which I wanted to get to, but didn't. In writing this book, I just completely reinvented my creative process in a lot of ways. One of the main things is that I've always line edited as I go. I could spend, like, hours on a paragraph, which is just painful. But with this, I had such a tight deadline, and I had was so limited on time—like, personal time—to do it that my mantra just became, "embrace urgency and imperfection."

And it was really a process of just vomiting words onto a page. The writer Jami Attenberg does this thing called "1,000 Words of Summer," where you write 1,000 words a day for two weeks. So, I did that. And then I just kept going. I was getting up early. It was fortunate that I tried this during the summer because it would have been hard in the winter. But I was getting up at, like, 5:30 a.m., before my family got up, and trying to write a thousand words a day. At that point, I was thinking, "it's very possible that I will do nothing else in terms of book writing during this time, but at least I'll have done this." At that stage, I wasn't thinking about what chapter I was writing or even about what the book as a whole was going to be. It was more like, "here's an idea that I have, and I'm just going to write and see what happens." I sort of tricked myself into writing about sex because I had this hesitation, like, "I'm going to need to write about my own experience and what is it that I want to say?" And so on some of those mornings, for like a solid week, I was just seeing what would come out.

Because it was just for me. And I told myself it didn't have to end up in the book. Anyway, the sort of stuff like what you mentioned, about making out, arose out of that. And like, God, I honestly wish I could go back to being a 14-year-old and making out for fucking hours, right? It's just… that's what I want. I want to be lost in that total, amorphous crazy. It's so insane. And I don't think I can get it back. I mean, you could do, like, molly—and I have tried that to sort of recreate the experience. It comes close, but it's just not the same. Even so, I think people should try that. I'm not against it. In fact, I'm very for it. So that scene emerged from my practice of writing just for myself, and I started to wonder, like, "why does my body remember that experience and that boy?" It was crazy. I didn't know it was there. And again, I wasn't necessarily going to put it in the book. This was just to see if I could do it.

In the second half of the book, I was trying to boil everything down to neat chapters, and to identify the fundamental elements I'm thinking about when it comes to mothers and children. And basically, there's just no way around sex. We never talk about it, but it's the reason we're all here. Why do we want to have sex? Because it feels good, right? I mean, it should. That's what it's for—pleasure. And especially, like, a female body is designed for pleasure. So then after I wrote the scene with the making out, I wanted to try some other things.

And then I think it was a year after that camping trip that I described in the book. It was really amazing because that moment was so powerful for me, and it was a total paradigm shift. And I knew it when it was happening. And it was like a year later, I was like, Let me just try and remember that, because I think it also like, it just improved our connection, our relationship. It made me feel better in my body. It made him feel better in his body. And so then I was like, See? And then I wrote it, and I was like, I might see, right? That was in my first draft that I sent to Jen Graves. I was a little anxious, but she said I pulled it off, which was reassuring. I was like, OK, but there are no guidelines, right? I had read an essay by Melissa Febos in the Sewanee Review called "Mind Fuck," which is all about writing better sex, and that was something that gave me the courage to not use certain words.

You can describe it in any way. So, I decided, "I'm just going to write it how I want to write it." Febos totally gets a shout out for making me feel like I could try. And the whole time I was writing, I was thinking, "there's no rule that I have to include this," but at the same time it just felt so... true. You know what I mean? And it was so real to me that I started to think, "how can I not include this?" Like, "this is probably some of the realest shit that I've written for this book." I kept telling myself that I could take it out at any time. But then also, one thing that I have heard from so many people is that my writing has made them feel less alone. It's a great gift to hear that. But knowing that made me think there was value in sticking my neck out here. And it does feel like a risk in some ways, but I just knew that there would be people out there who are dealing with this.

The idea that we have a static sex drive or a static sexual identity is just such bullshit. So too is the idea that we have to follow some sort of script when it comes to sex. Getting rid of those constraints, I think, can be so liberating for people who, say, can't always get it up. Or people who might have sexual problems stemming from antidepressants. We all go through these things, and it's very disorienting, and it's private in many ways, but it affects how we show up publicly and how we feel about ourselves. And I think it's so important, that idea of letting go again and just being the people we are, and being free to define sex however we want—because sex is whatever the fuck we want it to be. Yeah. In the end, it seemed it was worth it to include all that. I knew I had to do it, and I'm glad that I did.

Becker

Yeah. I'm incredibly grateful that you did. And were you saying about Melissa Febos, that essay made you feel like you could try? I just feel that about both of you so much. Like, the two of you, specifically, are people who make me feel that what I want to do is possible.

Garbes

Yeah. And it is. You just have to keep trying. I mean, that's the other thing. I have to keep working on it, too. There were some other sex things that did not make it in the book. When I read them later, I was thinking, "well, that's bad." But then for other things, I was like that's not bad. The passage I'm thinking of was something about the pandemic, about feeling this urgency I didn't realize until afterwards.

A lot of this book is really about me defining myself, to myself. That's what I was doing. It's definitely the most free I've ever felt in writing anything. I was like, "let me just try things." I had been living under these conditions where I wondered if I would ever write again. So, I just felt like, if I'm going to do it, let's just fucking do it, you know? Let's just fucking go for it and see what happens. And that's a lot of the spirit of the book. That's how the book was written. If I had been holding on to ideas of what I thought I could or couldn't do, then I'm not sure I would have been able to write it.

I was kind of writing myself free. The book is, in many ways, a love letter to my Filipina American heritage and identity. And I decided really early on in the writing process that I've been explaining myself to white people forever, and I'm just not going to do that anymore. Like, the things that are part of my culture, they can stand on their own. There will be no explanatory commas. There will be no italicization. And it's just like, if people want, they can still look it up. And isn't that beautiful to engage someone in that way?

Becker

Yes, it is. Well, I think we'll wrap it up there. Thank you so much for this incredible conversation.

Garbes

Oh, my God, you're so welcome. Thank you for wanting to talk to me. Let's keep talking.

Little North Fork
Joe Wilkins

When the rains finally came
the slope—clearcut a decade back,
fire-stripped this past September—

slid into the river.
Like the round mouths of storms
or the salmon's loose eye,

topsoil and ash turned an hour
in the current. And what was
went away.

*Floating logging camp at Hope, B.C., 1950. Decco-Walton Logging Company.
City Light Negatives (Record Series 1204-01), Seattle Municipal Archives.*

Contributors.

Nanya Jhingran *(Remaindered)* is a poet, scholar and teacher from Lucknow, India currently living by the coastal margin of the Salish Sea, on the unceded lands of the Coast Salish People (upon which the city of Seattle was built). She is an Associate Editor at *Poetry Northwest*, where she edits the book reviews section. Her recent work can be found or is forthcoming in *Seventh Wave*, *Poetry Northwest*, and *Honey Literary*, among others.

Matt Briggs *(Old Ladies of the Woods)* is a writer from the Pacific Northwest. His essay "Falling and Always Falling: *Twin Peaks* and the Clear-Cut Landscape" appeared in *Moss: Volume One*. His short stories have been published in *The Seattle Review*, *StringTown*, the *Chicago Review*, and elsewhere. He is the author of eight works of fiction, including the novel *Shoot the Buffalo*, which was nominated for a Washington State Book Award and won the Before Columbus Foundation's American Book Award. Briggs grew up in the Snoqualmie Valley and currently live in Des Moines, Washington.

Kim Fu *(#ClimbingNation)* is the author of the story collection *Lesser Known Monsters of the 21st Century*. Fu's first novel, *For Today I Am a Boy*, won the Edmund White Award for Debut Fiction and was a finalist for the PEN/Hemingway Award. Her second novel, *The Lost Girls of Camp Forevermore*, was a finalist for the Washington State Book Awards. Fu's writing has appeared in *Granta*, the *Atlantic*, the *New York Times*, and *BOMB*. She lives in Seattle.

Keygan S. S. McClellan *(Machines)*, a naturalist and graduate of the Creative Writing and Environment MFA program at Iowa State University, explores the confluence between nonhuman and human. Her writing appears in *The Iowan*, *Cleaver Magazine*, the climate fiction anthology *Nothing Is As It Was*, *Cold Mountain Review*, and other publications.

Jory Mickelson *(Reading the Book of Isaiah While Wild Fires Continue to Burn)* is a writer whose work has appeared or is forthcoming in *Court Green*, *Mid-American Review*, *The Rumpus*, *Ninth Letter*, and other journals. They are the recipient of an Academy of American Poet's Prize and have received fellowships from the Lambda Literary Foundation and The Helene Wurlitzer Foundation of New Mexico. Their first full-length collection *WILDERNESS//KINGDOM* is the inaugrual winner of the Evergreen Award Tour from Floating Bridge Press and a 2020 High Plains Book Award Finalist. They live in the Pacific Northwest.

Katherine D. Morgan *(Glory Glory Hallelujah)* is author of the debut chapbook *No Self-Respecting Woman*. Her work has appeared or is forthcoming at *Huffington Post*, *Bitch Media*, *LitHub*, *The Rumpus*, and *Hello-Giggles*, among others. Katherine's work has been nominated for the two Best of Net awards. She lives in Portland, Oregon, where she works at Powell's Books.

Aaron Fullerton *(Dash)* is a Los Angeles-based writer for film, television, and other mediums. He grew up on a small island in the Puget Sound and graduated from the University of Southern California's Writing for Film and Television program with honors. He has developed projects with companies such as Amblin, MRC, Appian Way, and Wondery, and has written for and produced a variety of one-hour shows, most recently *Happy Face*, which will air on Paramount+ next year.

Shin Yu Pai *(Monuments for Men (Memory's Vault), Fort Worden)* is the author of several books of poetry, including *Virga, ENSŌ, Sightings: Selected Works (2000-2005), Aux Arcs, Adamantine*, and *Equivalence*. She served as the fourth poet laureate of the City of Redmond, Washington, from 2015 to 2017. She is a three-time fellow of MacDowell and has completed residencies at Taipei Artist Village, Centrum, and The Ragdale Foundation. She writes, hosts, and produces the podcast *The Blue Suit* for KUOW Public Radio.

María de Lourdes Victoria *(A La Fuerza)* es una autora bilingüe cuyas obras han sido galardonadas y editadas internacionalmente en inglés y en español. Oriunda de Veracruz, México, María radica y escribe en Washington y California donde también imparte talleres de narración. María es fundadora de Seattle Escribe, la organización más numerosa de escritores que escriben en español en el estado de Washington. Actualmente escribe su cuarta novela y una colección de cuentos.

Maria de Lourdes Victoria *(A La Fuerza)* is a bilingual, award winning author whose work has been published internationally in English and Spanish. A native from Veracruz, Mexico, Maria lives and writes in Washington and California where she also teaches narrative workshops. Maria is the founder of Seattle Escribe, the largest organization of writers who write in Spanish in the state of Washington. She is currently writing her fourth novel and a collection of short stories.

Max Delsohn *(The Bubble)* is a writer whose work appears in or is forthcoming from *McSweeney's Quarterly Concern, VICE, The Rumpus, Nat. Brut, Passages North*, and *Triangle House*, among other places. They have been awarded residencies and fellowships from the Constance Saltonstall

Foundation for The Arts, Mineral School, and Hugo House. They are currently an MFA candidate in fiction at Syracuse University.

Jaye Nasir *(Prayer for Trimet Line 17)* lives in Portland, OR where she spends her time writing fiction, nonfiction and poetry that blurs, or outright ignores, the line between the real and the unreal. Her work has appeared or is forthcoming in *Buckmxn Journal, Santa Clara Review, Lammergeier Magazine, Mud Season Review, Phantom Kangaroo*, and elsewhere.

Jennifer Fernandez *(Cabin Life)* is a Cuban-American writer. Her short stories have appeared in several literary journals and her creative nonfiction piece, "The Cuban Brown Rabbit" was nominated for a Pushcart Prize in 2021. She lives near Seattle, Washington.

David Naimon *(Still Living Things)* is a writer in Portland, Oregon and host of the literary podcast *Between the Covers*. He is also the co-author, with Ursula K. Le Guin, of *Ursula K. Le Guin: Conversations on Writing*, a Hugo award finalist and winner of the 2019 Locus award in nonfiction. His writing can be found in *Orion, AGNI, Boulevard, Black Warrior Review*, and *Tin House*. It has received a Pushcart prize, been reprinted in *The Best Small Fictions* and been cited in *Best American Mystery & Suspense, Best American Travel Writing* and *Best American Essays*. He is currently finishing a genre-resistant collection of stories, essays and poems.

CMarie Fuhrman *(Door Stoop)* is the author of the poetry collection *Camped Beneath the Dam* and co-editor of *Native Voices: Indigenous Poetry, Craft, and Conversations*. Her poetry and nonfiction has been published, or is forthcoming, in several journals and anthologies. CMarie is a regular columnist for the *Inlander*, Translations Editor for Broadsided Press, and Director of the Elk River Writers Workshop. She is Director of Poetry at Western Colorado University, where she also teaches Nature Writing. CMarie is 2021-2023 Idaho Writer in Residence.

Ayana Harscoet [they/them] *(Futures)* is a queer, diasporic Japanese- and French-American poet based in unceded Duwamish territory (Seattle, WA). An emerging writer and recent college grad, they're currently chasing after / compelled by / diving into rivers, ecological restoration, and the limits of western science.

Rita Sturam Wirkala *(La Forestal)* is an award-winning Argentine writer and educator living in Seattle. After years of academic writing and teaching at the University of Washington, she now writes novels, short stories, children's poetry, and literary reviews, and works with emerging writers teaching classes and creative writing workshops. Her work has been published in Spain, Argentina, and the United States and has won praise from major Spanish-language newspapers. She holds a PhD in Spanish Literature.

Alex Vigue *(Boys of Boise 1955)* is a queer writer from Vancouver, Washington. He has a bachelor's degree in creative writing from Western Washington University and has been recently published in *Peach Mag*, *Chronotope*, and *Homology Lit*. His debut chapbook "The Myth of Man" was published by Floating Bridge Press.

Joe Wilkins *(Little North Fork)* is author of the novel, *Fall Back Down When I Die*, which was a finalist for both the Center for Fiction's First Novel Award and the Pacific Northwest Book Award, and a winner of the 2020 High Plains Book Award. Wilkins is also the author of a memoir, *The Mountain and the Fathers*, winner of a 2014 GLCA New Writers Award, and four collections of poetry, including *Thieve* and *When We Were Birds*, winner of the Oregon Book Award. Born and raised in eastern Montana,

Wilkins lives with his family in the Yamhill Valley of Oregon, where he directs the creative writing program at Linfield University.

Moss is represented for film/TV by **Alexandra Kordas** at 42 Management & Productions.

Moss was founded by **Connor Guy**, a book editor based in New York, and **Alex Davis-Lawrence**, a filmmaker based in Los Angeles. Both were born and raised in Seattle.

*M*oss.

A journal of the Pacific Northwest.

Editors
Connor Guy
Alex Davis-Lawrence

Managing Editor
Alayna Becker

Contributing Editors
Sharma Shields
Kailee Haong
Steven L. Moore
Michael Chin
M. Allen Cunningham
Diana Xin

Poetry Editors
Dujie Tahat
Ashley Toliver
Jalayna Carter

Creative Director
Alex Davis-Lawrence

Director of Outreach
Amy Wilson

Programming Coordinator
Cali Kopczick

Additional Design
Ilana Davis-Lawrence

Readers
McKenzie Watson-Fore
Rachel Lincoln Sarnoff
Jamie Bail
Elissa Favero
Paisley Green
Sasheem Silkiss-Hero
Kimm Stammen
Angelica Lai

Escalators in central library, 1960.
City Light Negatives (Record Series 1204-01), Seattle Municipal Archives.

Acknowledgments.

Moss is proud to be a subscriber-supported journal. We owe an ongoing debt of gratitude to all our readers, writers, and subscribers—particularly our Patrons, whose exceptional annual support makes our work possible:

Diann Barry and Mark Guy
Thomas and Elizabeth Beck
Max Boyd
Aaron Brown
Alba Conte
Diane Davis
Susan Davis
Ronnie-Gail Emden
Naomi Gibbs
Joe Grube
Kris Hattori and Melanie Lim
Paul Lawrence and Cynthia Jones
Sarah Lawrence
Kimberly Roque and Michael Chan
Ann Stinson
Anna and David Straka
Amanda Wong
Aria Woods
Kaye and Robert Woods

Interested in subscribing?

*Visit **mosslit.com** to support Northwest writing
and get the annual print edition delivered to your door.*